YOU TAKE THE
HIGH ROAD
and I'll take
        the bus!

YOU TAKE THE HIGH ROAD
and I'll take the bus!

Celebrating mediocrity in a world that tries too hard

Carrie Cox

ALLEN&UNWIN

Allen & Unwin
83 Alexander Street
Crows Nest NSW 2065
Australia
Phone: (61 2) 8425 0100
Fax: (61 2) 9906 2218
Email: info@allenandunwin.com
Web: www.allenandunwin.com

National Library of Australia
Cataloguing-in-Publication entry:

Cox, Carrie, 1972– .
    You take the high road and I'll take the bus : celebrating
    mediocrity in a world that tries too hard.

    ISBN 1 74114 397 7.

    1. Australian wit and humour. I. Title.

A827.3

Set in 11/14 pt Minion by Midland Typesetters, Maryborough, Victoria
Printed by Griffin Press, Netley, South Australia
10 9 8 7 6 5 4 3 2 1

Contents

For Coxy, Emily, Lara
and the Gipper

And when things start to happen,
Don't worry. Don't stew.
Just go right along.
You'll start happening too.
    Dr Seuss (1904–91), *Oh the places you'll go!*

Acknowledgements

Thanks a bunch to whichever author first introduced the self-indulgence of an acknowledgements section.

Thanks also to my publisher, Jo Paul, who didn't baulk at the idea of a book about mediocrity nor at the prospect of working with a writer who embraced it. And to Joanne Holliman for holding my sweaty hand throughout the production process.

Thanks to newspaper editors John Schalch, Mitchell Murphy and Eileen Rothwell, all champions, who grant me weekly column space and pay my pathetic-looking homemade invoices. Thanks especially to David Cavenagh, who gave me my very first column well before it was warranted.

Thanks many times over to Mara Lee, former editor of *Practical Parenting* magazine and an author in her own right.

Thanks sincerely to Mum for encouraging us to be creative and to generate our own ideas, to Dad for first suggesting that I lower my expectations and for his humour, and to my family en masse for routinely putting the 'fun' in dysfunctional.

Carrie Cox

Introduction

Ever tried writing a book? It's a dog of a project to undertake and I'll be buggered if I'll do it again. Seriously, it takes ages. For the life of me I can't work out how other writers do it more quickly and can only assume they let every other aspect of their lives fall by the wayside in the meantime—certainly an admirable approach if you don't mind being an unlikable git with permanent trackie pant welts.

It's highly likely you're reading this book in a library (why people pay for books I'll never understand), and that this library is one of maybe three in Australia to stock the book (by way of government donation), and that in fact only two copies of the book have been legitimately sold in a manner that requires the handing over of money. I'll write both off for tax. In which case, this book will have been an outstanding success, because not only did I finish the back-grabbing monkey of a thing while also juggling a child or two, relationship, career, home, financial responsibilities, flailing friendships, a demonically possessed computer, and the depressing state of world affairs, but I also managed to get it published—which was, at the end of the day, my primary goal.

Yes, somewhere between abject failure and outright success is where I'm pitching things these days; somewhere very close to mediocre. It's this nice little place where you can feel good about yourself for achieving doable goals, for simply existing without going completely mad, even while those about you are forever demanding that you jump higher, reach further, dig deeper and earn more.

You take the high road and I'll take the bus is my attempt to reclaim the sullied reputation of mediocrity as a benchmark of relative success. For too long mediocrity has copped an unfair rap. Its very definition has been twisted and tainted by a world that tries too hard. To not covet conventional measures of success these days, and ergo happiness, is to 'wallow in mediocrity', to 'slide into obscurity', or to generally flail about like an abandoned duck in life's quagmire of failure—as though these are bad things.

This book redefines both success and mediocrity by aligning a life more ordinary with a truer measure of happiness—a big, shrug-of-the-shoulders kind of happiness born of acceptance, inevitability, a little piss-taking and much back-slapping all round. It recognises that whether you choose to either laugh at or applaud mediocrity, the concept has long been underrated as a source of great enjoyment and progress.

This is the real person's guide to getting by in this difficult thing called life, ostensibly by laughing at the hurdles, life stages, people, awkward situations, impossible expectations and sheer ridiculousness that inevitably clutter the way. It argues that basic survival and so-called mediocrity are not only big asks . . . they're outstanding achievements! The frightfully ordinary among us should be profiled, recognised and celebrated, as many of them are herein.

Sage advice? Wrong book. Self-help? Back of the store. Rather, I offer you within these pages a series of essays and observations to merely make you smirk occasionally and ponder momentarily while avoiding exercise and waiting for that ship to finally come in.

Some of these musings have been extracted from columns I've written for various newspapers and magazines over the years, but let's not trouble ourselves with copyright issues this early in the day. Most, however, have been tapped out exclusively for this book. I don't expect you to read them all (hell, when was the last time you got to finish anything?), but I do expect you to pat yourself on the back for at least trying.

What do we WANT!
Mediocrity.
When do we want it?!
Whenever.

This book doesn't have a complimentary fridge magnet, though Lord it should. The humble fridge magnet is the one thing the marketing gurus behind the self-help movement got right—cheap, simple and strangely magnetic . . . a lot like my husband really. So I've done my own but, sorry, you'll have to photocopy it first, then find a magnet, then get some glue, then . . .

Chapter 1

Don't worry, what's happy?

So I wanted to write a book about mediocrity. In fact, I wanted to call it *Mediocrity: a user's guide*. But then you probably wouldn't have bought that book.

You wouldn't have bought that book because mediocrity is widely viewed as a negative term and when you feel negative you don't want to read a book that might make you feel worse than you already do. Far preferable, then, to gravitate on over to the exclamation marks section of the bookstore, the section that promises: *You can do anything*! *You are not a loser*!! *Ultimate happiness is just a few deep breaths and a fundamental philosophical shift away*!!! There you will find everything your life is lacking, every step to success you forgot to take, every harbinger of happiness, every rationale for failure, every profile of a person who's already achieved so much more than you have.

You will buy one of these books because it promises to make you better! Stronger! Fitter! Richer! Wiser! Worthier! All those exclamation marks can't be for nought! Doing this will count as a positive step in the right direction. A step away from everything you are now; everything your punch-drunk life has become. I mean, isn't it just *possible* that the secrets to success and happiness could be a mere $29.95 away?

Well, they might. They certainly might. God knows Louise Adams' *Feel the fear and do it anyway*! gave my mother the courage to reverse park after years of circling shopping centres waiting for everyone to go home. There's a lot to be said for self-help, especially its basic premise that at the end of the day the only person you can rely upon to comfortably adjust yourself is . . . you.

But there's a lot to be said for self-justification too, though not presently in polite company. In a world that simply doesn't dish up equal servings of good fortune, emotional security, opportunities or inoffensive nose shapes, it's plainly wrong to assert that a red-hot go at self-help will deliver life's booty in spades.

My humble campaign for mediocrity rests on the simple Einsteinian principle that for every action there is an equal and opposite reaction: keep pushing people to better themselves and you'll only serve to remind them how crap they are. Push the bar higher, we'll only feel lower on the ground.

And what's so wrong with us anyway? Is everyone else *really* so much happier and more successful than we are? Are we truly just one of the unlucky ones? Or does it simply look that way from the perenially slow checkout lane?

What do we even know about happy and successful? Is that pleasurable moment when you knock the top off your sixth beer during the Friday night footy *really* happiness? Or does it just smell like it? Is success something that can be measured by money or status? Then where does that leave Mother Teresa? Fred Hollows? Anyone who's helped save humanity without sending an invoice?

The point is, if we knew what happy and successful really were, we wouldn't be constantly chasing them, dodging them, meditating on them, studying them, workshopping them and generally suspecting that everyone bar us has them. We'd have pinned them down, toasted the spoils and organised a testimonial dinner by now. Game over.

But of course the real appeal of happy and successful is their sheer elusiveness. They're always but one more holiday, two Lotto wins and three self-help books away. We're not even completely sure what they look like, although that woman with the flippy ponytail who hosts *Changing rooms* seems awfully close.

All we *do* know about happy and successful is that we're supposed to be chasing them. For that is what we've always been told—by our parents, our teachers, our mentors, magazines and movies—since day one. Try harder kids! Study longer, jump further, reach higher! Come on, happy and successful can't be too far away now. You won't get them standing around pulling your sister's hair, you great git.

Yet who among life's many tutors actually has happy and successful in their grasp? Which of them can categorically prove they've attained life's Big Point? How can they prove that which can't fairly be measured?

And if so many ostensibly successful people are too busy peddling their bikes to realise they're supposed to be happy at the same time, then what is the point of riding anyway? Wouldn't the bus be a better option? Why is it so many people get to the end of their lives and wish they'd spent less time trying to find a park and more time simply hanging out at one? Are 'happy' and 'successful' too pure to exist, serving only to tease the imagination? Are they the impossibly beautiful people on the front cover of the brochure of life, resplendent in their matching white cossies as they sip mango daiquiris on the beach at sunset? (Come on, everyone knows mango would stain a white cossie.)

It seems to me there is a fundamental flaw with the general premise that parents should endeavour to rear happy, successful children. We're giving them and ourselves a bum steer by selling happy and successful as life's ultimate, one-and-the-same goals. Plenty of people mosey along perfectly well in life without ever coming close to conventional definitions of happy or successful. The rest of us mope around in varying states of disappointment—happy but not successful, successful but not happy, full but what if we'd ordered what the guy at the next table did?—forever convinced we're missing out on something.

But missing out on what? When was the last time someone who wasn't on smack came up to you with an idiotic grin on their face and said, 'I'm blissfully happy and wildly successful! I've got everything I ever wanted and more'? Or even, 'You know, I'm frequently satisfied with various aspects of my life and I'm not presently in jail. Could it be that I'm happy and successful?'

I'm guessing, not recently. In reality, none of us actually knows what happy and successful really are or precisely where our hopes and realisations might have already intersected. All we *do* know is what we've been led to believe so far, which is that giving up this existentialist struggle for ideals that are by definition always out of reach equates to *settling*. Equates to mediocrity.

This seemingly innate philosophy, embraced by each of us from a very young age, sets us up for a prolonged series of disappointments that we've collectively come to think of as 'life'. And look, it's all well and good up to a point, but is so much perpetual inadequacy *really* necessary? Does everything have to stink quite so much? Why is it that we're hellbent on purchasing anything and everything on offer that promises to 'make life easier' when our own personal default setting is stuck fast on doing everything the hard way?

What if an alternative perspective enabled you to keep a better focus on the things that matter, the things that don't, and the things that probably do but are really too much hassle?

What if there was a fourth window on *Playschool* that made the ordinary among us look brave and strong and the high-flyers look reckless and just plain silly? What if okay was really *okay*?

Let me introduce you to the first of my Mediocrity Hall of Fame entrants for those individuals, past and present, who earned success through mediocrity, who settled for mediocrity over successs, or who simply had mediocrity thrust upon them.

Mediocrity Hall of Fame
Life member: Stephen Bradbury

'The last shall be first,' the Holy Bible advises us. And so it came to pass that an ordinary ice skater from sunny Queensland outbalanced the best in the world to become the first ever Australian to win a Winter Olympics gold medal.

In what remains one of the most bizarre races in Olympic history, Stephen Bradbury became the good guy who finished first; the embodiment of the old adage that good things really do come to those who wait.

And wait he did. Way back in last place, as the American champion, his Chinese rival, a Korean and a Canadian all carved up the ice ahead of him. Bradbury's race plan was simple: 'I was shooting for a bronze and just trying to stay out of trouble at the back because there'd been so many crashes in the competition already'.

But even in the fickle world of ice skating, Bradbury could never have imagined what would happen next. As the Chinese skater tried to pass the American, he clipped his skate and the pair hit the deck together, producing a jumble of skates and helmets and pained expressions that proved the undoing of the skaters behind.

All except Stephen Bradbury, who was skating his little heart out at a far enough distance away that negotiating a path around the melee was simply a matter of staying upright and minding one's step.

'I was never expecting the whole field to go down and leave me the only one standing', Stephen explained. (In fact he'd emailed the American competitor the day before the race to remind him, when crossing the finish line first, to wear the skates Stephen had supplied him bearing Bradbury's company logo.) 'But at the end of the day I won the race. I was the only guy who stayed on his feet. I consider myself the luckiest man. God smiles on you some days and this was my day'.

Indeed, life dispenses justice in peculiar ways. Perhaps after a lifetime devoted to a sport in which he would probably never be the world's best, after whipping national speed records in a nation that didn't care, after three disappointing Olympics results, after countless shattering disqualifications, and after a near-death accident that once saw him lose four litres of blood on the sharp end of a skate, Bradbury had earned his day in the sun.

Yes, mediocrity can shine like success on a good day. And life's champions can be those who just keep showing up.

The unbearable lightness of being conned

Come on now, be honest. It hasn't all gone to plan, has it? Those dreamy ideas you hatched that summer as you lay back on your Garfield doona taping the Top Forty off the radio and watching the sun's rays make love heart shapes on your ceiling as your father screamed at you to turn that *goddamned* music down and take this pile of *crap* out of the doorway—they just haven't come off, have they?

The grand love affair, the outrageously successful career, the high-powered revenge against everyone who ever made you feel second-rate, the inspired reversal of all your parents' mistakes, the early financial windfall, the exotic travel years, the great invention, the movie deal, the latent discovery of obscene musical talent, the blossoming of your unsightly head into a swan-like structure, the impossibly magnificent home on acreage, the gorgeous and abnormally well-behaved children . . . feel free to stop me anytime here . . . they've almost all failed to eventuate, haven't they? Not in a tragic, my-life-is-a-train-wreck kind of way, of course—no, that would have given you fodder for a book about something other than the celebration of your ordinariness—but more in a steady, rust-formation fashion: the gentle collapse of one great expectation into the next.

Everything's ended up kind of average, far from stellar and impressive, and your neck is sore from straining to see another contemporary whiz by in the jetstream of happiness and success. Where did your train slide so sneakily off track? When did life start getting in the way of your dreams? How did it all get so hard? Would a decent lie-down be out of the question?

You've started believing you're simply not one of the special ones, right? That, contrasted with the success you'd once dreamt of and the models of success thrown at you daily, you're nothing but ordinary after all. Perhaps even . . . mediocre.

And would you get a grip already?!! Contrary to everyone who is wrong, mediocrity is *not* the antithesis of success. It is not the opposite of accomplishment, a hiding ground for hopelessness, nor even the name of the last decent pub open in Loserville. In fact, it is a modern tragedy that mediocrity has come to be looked upon with such raw disdain by social commentators. It's become the fresh turd on the shoe of relative success—something one inadvertently stands in or, worse, falls headlong into.

But it hasn't always been this way. Throughout history, mediocrity has in fact endured a see-sawing reputation, at times revered by great sociological observers as the most natural state of being for humankind, and a bloody good idea at that.

'Not being the worst stands in some rank of praise', suggested William Shakespeare after a particularly rough day on the quill. And he should know. Poor Shakes never felt real success in his day—it was almost all posthumous—and in fact his time on earth was a fairly pedestrian, lacklustre affair, punctuated by a marriage break-up and the odd sexuality crisis.

Oscar Wilde, too, was a man whose success belied a healthy respect for mediocrity. He vacillated greatly between wanting to change the world and simply changing his sheets on the one hand, commenting that 'The one duty we owe history is to rewrite it', while on the other insisting that 'Life is far too important to be taken seriously'. In the end Wilde settled for the latter philosophy, winding down his days in a state of wry bemusement in a grotty French hotel room, just three years after he was finally released from prison for being a 'ponce'—well before it was fashionable.

'A man is a success if he gets up in the morning and gets to bed at night, and in between does what he wants to do', said Muhammad Ali, or possibly Bob Dylan. Either way, it's yet another pithy observation that I have plundered from history to illustrate my point that success and mediocrity have been happy bedfellows at times, even if success did sleep with one eye on the doorknob.

Yes, mediocrity hasn't always been a dirty word. It hasn't always been associated with abject failure and half-arsed efforts. As Chapter 6 clearly shows, the entire history of the world can be looked upon through a viewfinder of mediocrity if we're happy to accept this book's revised definition of mediocrity as thus:

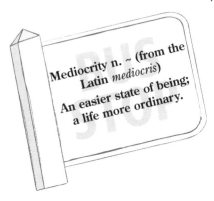

Mediocrity n. ~ (from the Latin *mediocris*) An easier state of being; a life more ordinary.

Go photocopy it and whack it on the fridge now.

Indeed, all was going swimmingly for mediocrity until about halfway through last century. The pursuit of a life more ordinary had been tacitly raised at various junctures by those wise enough to recognise its many natural benefits—chief among them: moderate happiness, self-acceptance and regular sleep-ins—and the battle-weary post-war population was starting to embrace the idea of simple pleasure. *I'm OK, you're OK* wrote some dangerously mellow author from his Jason recliner.

Then, circa 1980, everything went to hell in a handbasket. The whole world shuddered out of third gear and into first, unshackling the hangover of the sixties (aka the seventies) and embracing new technologies and priorities to bust open family units, scour the skies for spare change and hurtle towards financial nirvana before the Cold War froze us all. Greed became the new black,

Mediocrity Hall of Fame
Life member: Bob Dylan

Bob Dylan became famous because he rejected the ideals of success thrown at him by 1960s' culture: the white-picket fence, the 2.1 kids, the rifle-bought privacy. But in a beautifully mediocre spin, he then casually shattered the hopes of his ageing hippy fan club when he revealed all in his 2004 memoirs. 'The world was absurd', he said of the 60s' uprising. 'I had very little in common with and knew even less about a generation that I was supposed to be the voice of.

'I was actually fantasising about a nine-to-five existence, a house on a tree-lined block with a white picket fence, pink roses in the backyard.'

And of the diehards who turned up to pay homage to his family home in Woodstock, Dylan said: 'I wanted to set fire to those people.'

Seems the times they were a-changing…

success was an empty briefcase, and mediocrity was the bus route to obscurity.

To recover from the eighties, and the rude shock that we were all still alive save for our stock portfolios, the nineties delivered the self-help movement. This, it was promised, would make all of us feel a whole lot better about ourselves, wrestling back the remote control from whichever one of our inner personalities was blocking the path to our rebirth with a pile of bad crystals.

In its infancy, the self-help movement was a quaint, musk-smelling, harmless phenomenon; a few deep breaths between friends. Insidiously, however, its commercial trade and influence expanded from incense-filled corner shops and market stalls to the cashed-up and stress-weary corporate world. Post-it Note affirmations grew like topsy into half-day seminars, thought-per-page book series, lunchtime yoga classes and, inevitably, the corporate retreat.

Corporate retreats especially have a lot to answer for. Once was the time when a job was a job, and the stuff that came before and after it was life. It didn't matter how physically fit, emotionally balanced or spiritually nurtured you were, as long as you turned up, cleaned your own coffee cup and didn't leave before your shout on Friday arvo. Then the corporate world swallowed life entirely, figuring that fit, balanced, chakra-stroking men and women are far more happy and productive little vegemites, capable of producing oodles more profit for the company for a larger portion of their natural lives.

Last year I waved goodbye to my husband as he set off on an eleven-day corporate 'boot camp'. Its aim, apparently, was to restore a sense of balance to his life; to remind him about the things that really matter, as opposed to those that don't like, say, family and weekends.

Far from enjoying himself, my husband assured me he would be working around the clock, pushing his physical boundaries (which had previously stopped at the fridge), abandoning bad habits (including—yes!—smoking) and developing a 'Life Plan'. He said all of this without laughing.

I was dismayed to be losing my husband for so long, especially as we lived in a city with no family around us, but I was relieved to discover that I had largely forgotten about him by day three.

When he finally returned, it was with an extra suitcase full of textbooks (*Corporate kumbaya*, vols 1–56) and a fresh resolve to transform his entire life. From now on, explained my husband, he would be drinking approximately four hundred litres of water a day and he suggested I do the same. (I declined, realising that one of us would actually have to be *out* of the toilet to let the landlord in when he came to evict us.)

Secondly, he said, there would be much yoga-like activity in the house and that I wasn't to snigger, no matter how much he inadvertently flatulated while crouching in the Dragon Stance.

Finally, my husband read me his Life Plan, a simple series of dot points that would progressively lead him towards a better-rounded, healthier, more satisfying life; one in which work and home sat perfectly balanced on life's big see-saw.

And then he went outside for a smoke.

It could be argued that, by not believing for one minute that my spouse would sustain any long-term life improvements as a result of a corporate retreat, I did not create an environment conducive to his success. Ha! I too have thrown myself into the depths of corporate motivational programs, huffed, puffed and blown my psychological barriers down, brainstormed, barn-stormed and transformed, only to emerge unchanged, uninspired and frankly unimpressed.

In fact, I have even knelt at the feet of The Guru, one of Australia's most revered motivational experts, a man hired only by those companies big enough to afford him and too busy to check his credentials. Rhett Starr, for that's what we'll call him, is the personification of every self-help book ever written. And for a mere $10 000 a day (not including tea and coffee and those addictive little bowls of mints), he will 'Change The Way You Think'.

Rhett does this by revealing the little-known secret that God thought it best to share with Rhett only: that there are Rules Of

Life, and that if we obey these to the letter, great success will rain down in buckets. These are the rules Rhett shared with me:

RULE 1   The only person who can effectively solve your problems is you. (Unfortunately, this means Rhett is unable to offer a money-back guarantee for his services.)

RULE 2   If you want to do something, you have to learn how. (Unless it's ripping off delusional CEOs with flaky self-help courses, which is frankly a doddle.)

RULE 3   When you look for the solutions to your problems in other people or situations, you're looking in the wrong place. (They're actually down the back of the couch where you left them.)

RULE 4   When you consciously improve another person's quality of life, you feel good. (Personally, I'm beside myself with joy that Rhett lives in a Double Bay mansion on account of schmucks like me.)

RULE 5   There is an upside and a downside to everything. (Gravity. Who knew?)

RULE 6   You can be anything you want to be. (It's true! Rhett was just a lowly vacuum cleaner salesman until he stumbled across his first self-help book. Now he's making squillions just by regurgitating other people's motivational clichés with a very earnest expression on his face and by getting you to do deep-breathing exercises whenever he forgets where he's up to.)

Even when you manage to dodge the shysters like Rhett (*I'm okay, You're okay, He's better than okay*), the great irony is that the whole self-help industry has actually done a stellar job of making most of us feel worse about ourselves—dramatically uncovering the rampant insecurities, unresolved issues and emotional flaws within all of us. Worse, it has convinced many of us that we are living hopelessly short of our potential—that true happiness exists in a place higher, further, faster, wiser, richer, deeper and more inaccessible by taxi than we ever might have suspected. The only way to find it is to keep looking inwards for personal flaws to fix, and to buy as many pithy fridge magnets as one possibly can.

And so it is at this juncture in time, the infancy of the new millennium, and with the world's default setting stuck fast on 'Try harder', that mediocrity has slipped below obscurity to become synonymous with simply not trying at all—an offensive brand of indifference acceptable only to supermodels. Once perched on the cusp of becoming a celebrated movement, mediocrity has instead come to be seen as a sorry excuse for existence; the very opposite of success.

But not for long! The rumblings of change have begun. A new movement is knocking at the door, or at least it's thinking about it. Heart-attack candidates are throwing in their high-flying jobs and hightailing it to the bush. Frazzled families are going on seaside holidays and not coming back. CEOs are job-sharing to free up time for getting the garden back up to scratch. (I could provide you with statistics, but that's hardly fun.)

The world is sighing, settling, ready to accept something less, something easier. They might not know it yet, but a happily more ordinary future exists for those willing to kick back, accept the inevitable, celebrate the mediocre, identify the shortest straight line between any two tasks and, most importantly, start flying beneath the radar of great expectations.

Hell, I'm not even going to spell-check this chapter.

Chapter 2

Great expectations

Blessed is he who expects nothing for he shall never be disappointed.
Jonathon Swift (1667–1745)

I came, I saw, can I go now?

The simple fact is we don't ask to be born. We are quite happy being nothing. The moment of conception is thrust upon us like a runny egg on a caesar salad: uncalled for and inextractable.

Yet from that mysterious moment, a thousand or more expectations are heaped upon our fragile zygote shoulders, the most pressing of which is that we will make a startling, photo-worthy appearance in about forty weeks' time.

As though we have a choice in the matter. Having grown quite accustomed to the warmest, most peaceful, doona-like setting imaginable, our bare naked bodies will be rudely expelled by the natural and impatient whims of our mother's cervix. Ready or not, here I flop.

As for being photo-worthy, again we are hamstrung. It's not as if the womb comes complete with a mirror and vanity basin. We don't know what the hell we look like in there—what particular combination of dodgy genes we've been left with—so how can we possibly be responsible for our appearance upon exit? How can we hope to avoid the spectre of our parents' veiled shock and disappointment simply because we happen to have ears the size of satellite dishes and a nose that looks suspiciously like the pool man's?

Yet every parent will peer with expectant wonder at the business end of the labour bed, desperate to know what their little one looks like and—let's be honest—hoping upon hope that in spite of the fact we've just been rolling about in goo and poo for nine months, we'll come out looking like an extra in a Heinz commercial.

I mean, give a slug a break!

It's no flippant quirk of language that the state of pregnancy is referred to as 'expecting'. Pregnant couples are the most expectant people on earth, reading up on every stage of our impending growth and development as though, well, our very lives depended upon it. 'At eighteen weeks, you'll feel your baby's first kick', instruct the textbooks. 'No kick? Your baby is either a slow-developer, a chronic introvert or has no legs to speak of. Hold off on the MCG life membership! We may have ourselves a doozey.'

It's seldom theorised but almost certainly true that this sort of in-utero pressure has a tremendous impact on our developing psyches, slowly and insidiously preparing us for the exponentially growing set of expectations that await us on the outside and for the many ways in which we will inevitably disappoint.

But let's not get ahead of ourselves. Birth itself is a miraculous event and it's only right that a new baby, having successfully dodged miscarriage, tragedy and all that wine its mother drank before realising she was up the duff, is the main star of the show. How amazing it must feel—if only we could remember—to first peer out of the birth canal and see a roomful of faces gazing down at us.

All too fleeting, though, is the sensation that we are the centre of the universe. Barely have we had our moment to bask in the glory of those strong overhead theatre lights than we are whisked away for the first of life's many measurements and comparisons. (Is it any wonder we stand a one in ten chance of developing an eating disorder by the time we reach high school when one of the first questions everyone wants to know is 'How much did it weigh?)

Things really kick into overdrive when, away from the watchful eyes of midwives and doctors and well-meaning relatives, new parents are free to take their little creation home and commence moulding. 'We have made it', the new family muses, 'now let's see what it can *do*.'

'Smile', the new parents coax us a few mere days into our new environs. 'Smile at me. Smile at them. Eat something solid. Roll over. Hold this. Rock on that. Clap hands. Wear this ridiculous ensemble. Follow that football team. Look cute. Stand up. I said stand up. Now walk.'

And you'd think it would be enough that we finally drag our nappy-weighted butts off the floor and into a standing position, but no—it's always *more*, isn't it?

'Do a dance. Love The Wiggles. Like your cousin. Grow more hair. Reveal a talent. Embrace day care. Make friends. Be funny. Be asleep. Be quiet.' Yes, the expectations game gets off to a cracking start during those formative years, well before we've developed the wherewithal or confidence to speak up for ourselves and demand a break. Well before we learn about free will and choice. Well before we can turn to our parents, God love 'em, and say: 'You know what? *No.* No, I think not. I think that I'm actually going to sit over here in the blocks corner for a while and wait for someone to appreciate me for who I am. A few months ago you were happy with a burp. Now it's just Perform! Perform! Perform!'

All too late we realise that great expectations have become part of who we are, cleaved to our sides since the finish line of the sperm race. By the age of about five, we are fully conditioned to believe that we exist on this earth primarily to impress and improve, that our parents know best, and that approval is king.

Personally, I think the odd shopping centre tanty is a fair exchange for that amount of undue pressure.

For whom the lunch bell tolls

Unfortunately it's what we learn next in life that really brings us unstuck. This is when our parents, somewhat reluctantly and with one eye on their vanishing mortality, hand our fragile little egos over to the school system. I have moulded it, they say, now you must crush it. Or as Prochnow put it: 'First you have to teach a child to talk. Then you must teach it to be quiet.'

Ostensibly, schooling is supposed to open our minds to the wonders of education; to the joys of learning, application, creativity and personal advancement. But of course there is just one lesson underpinning the universal school experience and it is this: *Life is hard. Get used to it!*

Tantalising us with colourful play equipment just outside the classroom window, teachers make it known from the start that nothing of any enjoyable value will come to us without hard work, sacrifice and regular moments of ritual humiliation. With each passing year of school, the price tag on happiness is hung higher and higher, preparing us for the apparent mortifying struggle that is adulthood. 'You'll appreciate this one day', they tell us. 'The trauma of calculus is nothing compared with the pain of having your first marketing proposal tossed in the bin by your supervisor and then watching them a month later pitch the same proposal to a high-level team of decision-makers who reward it with a $70K contract and a promotion. Brian, take that compass out of your nose before I . . .'

Don't get me wrong, I loved school. I loved its emphasis on regular mealtimes, its healthy respect for long holidays, and its willingness to give just about any nuf-nuf a go at shaping young minds. Indeed, when I think back to some of the teachers I had in my provincial hometown all those years ago, I realise how wonderful—and miraculous—it is to be alive at all.

There was Mr Diller, the grade three teacher who actually tossed my best buddy Trevor out of the window during maths one morning. In grade four, Mrs Sallingham made me eat half a tub of Clag glue after I was caught committing that compelling primary school act of peeling dried glue off the back of one's hand (in some countries, a sign of advanced intelligence).

Mr Bright, who was anything but, threw a javelin at me during physical education to prove to the grade nine class that it was too blunt to actually pierce skin. (He was wrong.) And of course there was Mr Broughton, a paragon of virtue and good health, who would puff on a packet of Winnie Reds each lesson and blow smoke rings in the face of any student who showed dissent. (He also made us watch *The Dirty Dozen* sixteen times during the course of one year, but never *Picnic At Hanging Rock*, upon which our final assessment was based.)

Earth to Education Inspector?!

These teachers, and many like them, were desperately unhappy campers who offset their hate for their job, its lousy pay and apparent lack of professional respect, with amusing acts of cruelty performed upon hapless children. *Adulthood*, their bitter expressions screamed at us, *is not a happy place.*

Is it any wonder, then, that so many kids seek to muck up throughout their school years? To make spitballs while the sun shines? And is this not perhaps the best preparation for an adulthood that promises to be full of hard work, deadlines, sacrifices, disappointments and pained facial expressions?

It's been both crushing and liberating to discover in recent years that the most successful and probably happiest of all my former school colleagues was a guy who would only turn up for class if the surf wasn't up and the mood wasn't down. Fun-loving Dion—the guy who'd call the strictest teachers in the school by their first names and spend two hours out of every three-hour maths exam drafting an elaborate essay about how the true value of pi was in the placement of the peas and sauce—had an almost prescient sense of what lay beyond our school years.

His own preparation for the hard work and sacrifice that later forged a mini hotel management empire in Europe and the Middle East was to take from school only that which wouldn't weigh him down on the journey: fond memories, solid friendships, a joke for every occasion and the basic structure for an essay on pretty much anything. The only anomaly in Dion's make-up is that he wasn't heir to a vast media empire.

In stark contrast, dorks like myself frittered away those school years on earnest discussions with indifferent teachers about ways to squeeze an extra half-mark out of my biology results, pimple dramas (I once had a desperate moment with Dad's orbital sander), brain-draining talks with careers counsellors, after-school maths tutoring, lunchtime library sessions by the thousand and more public speaking competitions than John Farnham has had tearful send-offs.

You don't realise how life-forming any of this is until you attend your first high school reunion. Just when you've finally begun to make your way in the world—having fully workshopped that humiliating incident at school camp, the inexplicable missing page of your last geography exam and the sight of your best friend snogging the boy you'd pursued unfailingly for the past five years—comes the call to revisit the scene of the crimes; to catch up on what everyone's been up to for the last ten years or so, reminisce about old times and, most importantly, see who's gotten fat.

The main trouble with school reunions is that they tend to be initiated by a small posse of people for whom high school was one long summer of slumber parties and tickle fights. Years of fruitless Clearasil applications, forty-degree classrooms and home-perming accidents have seemingly vanished from their memories. They look back only with fondness, awash in the rosy hue of nostalgia. (They also just happen to be at the peak of their self-grooming routine, raging love life and career status around the exact same time they have scheduled the big event. What a freakish coincidence!)

I hopelessly mistimed my own approach to my first major high school reunion, having planned to shed large portions of my butt cheeks in time for the big event (I'm now on target for November 2014). It had been a long time since I'd thought seriously about high school. Apart from a nasty scar where my head had collided with a makeshift hurdle in grade eleven, I felt high school's impact had largely dissipated with the passage of years.

Right up until I walked into that hideously decorated RSL function room.

Suddenly my adult life ceased to exist. I was right back in 1980-something, surrounded by the stereotypes of my youth—the sporting jocks, the flirty girls, the library geeks, the smokers, the brains, the musical types and the boys who wore their shorts around their earlobes.

No-one had changed! At least not in any way that seemed to matter. The cool people still gravitated toward the other cool people, the straights discussed *Star Trek* episodes over the non-alcoholic punch, and the fringe-dwellers like me—those people who never quite seemed to fit into any one group—circled the room's periphery like nervous observers.

Sure, some people had had large litters of children, some had gone on to pursue moderately interesting careers, but by and large not a single person had transcended their high school template. We each remained captive to our calling; prisoners of peer definitions.

But thank God we could now get pissed without being grounded!

Yet even getting royally trolleyed at my high school reunion didn't seem to dull the latent impact of all those great expectations, lost opportunities and unrequited crushes that defined those years. Okay, actually it did. But it didn't stop me from remembering the crushing comment of the night, directed by a high-kicking cheerleader straight at me: 'So Carrie . . . still making life difficult for yourself then?'

Hey! I wanted to protest. I'd thought it was *supposed* to be difficult! By making things hard for myself back then, I'd been readying myself for how hard it would be down the track. Or at least how hard I'd been told to *expect* it to be by all those miserable, underpaid, dissatisfied teachers.

And of course, life *does* get much harder down the track, exponentially and inevitably so. But by then we're legally entitled to a stiff drink at the end of a tough day, we'll hopefully have acquired a healthy sense of adult cynicism, we have the option of happy ordinariness at our disposal and there are some genuinely fine moments to be had amidst the mayhem.

If only there'd been a subject back in school that actually taught one how to recognise the serendipitous moments of childhood and adolescence as they occurred. Perhaps then, with the benefit of foresight as well as hindsight, we'd better know how to recognise such moments in adulthood.

Other subjects that should be taught at school

Networking 101

In which we glance forward to the apparent difficulty of meeting new people in adulthood by looking back to the untapped wisdom of preschoolers.

As any parent of a four-year-old will tell you, the key to throwing a great kids' birthday party is to invite a dozen children who may or may not know each other, let them loose within a defined area and toss in a few chocolate crackles for good measure. Within five minutes, they'll have introduced themselves, made friends, joined hands, compared notes on Barbie vehicles, and arranged sleepovers well into the next year.

By contrast, I went to a work-organised cocktail party last year that handed out oversized nuts and bolts to the male and female guests respectively so that we might then nervously shuffle our way around the room to find the person with the perfectly matching piece and commence contrived conversation. In case conversation proved tricky, we were given a list of potential topics, such as the relative advantages of property investment over a managed share fund and the likelihood of there being an interest rate correction within the next six months. I've had more fun paying parking fines.

This important school subject would fill the chasm that exists between the efficient simplicity of early childhood and the awkward chaos of early adulthood by addressing some of the following key questions: At what point in life does meeting new people become so elaborately complicated? Why is it so effortless for children and so embarrassing for grown-ups? And when does a tiny piece of raw fish atop a wholewheat crouton become a better serving suggestion than a chocolate crackle?

Applied popularity

In which we observe and analyse the post-school journeys of impossibly good-looking footy captains, formal debs with princess complexes, and self-promoting all-rounders who always manage to sell an inordinately large number of raffle tickets.

It's easy to be so intimidated by the white-hot glow of such individuals' popularity that we fail to see how our own relative social standing at school could ever translate into something resembling grown-up success. Yet history shows that while the world might seem to be the popular kids' oyster, seldom do they have the smarts to crack open the shell. Hopelessly unprepared for the ego hurdles, financial obstacles, emotional surprises and dodgy employers that define life in the real world, popular kids often come unstuck at the first rail, leaving the way open for those of us less enamoured with our own potential.

Yes, scratch the veneer of any fake-smiling suburban hairdresser or used car salesman and you'll find a former popular kid demanding to know what went wrong.

Society says 'Put your hands on your head'

And so we graduate from our parents' early expectations through to those heaped upon us by the school system until we find ourselves standing at the juncture of Been There Avenue and What Now? Street. Erm, where to from here?

Faced with the sudden burden of setting up our own goalposts on an unfamiliar paddock, most of us begin adulthood by grabbing onto as many societal expectations as we can. Dutifully, society, via the media and popular culture, has gone ahead and prepared a list of new and improved great expectations for us to readily adopt and pursue.

All my life, I always wanted to be someone. Now I see that I should have been more specific.

Jane Wagner

In a very serious nutshell, these collective expectations are killing more young adults than the perilous practice of crossing the road while text-messaging. The pressure to look good, get rich quick and 'have it all', ideally while enjoying a stint of minor celebrity, is all-consuming and has been cited by many behavioural psychologists as one of the key factors behind the alarming incidence of youth suicide in western nations.

In Australia today, suicide is the eighth leading cause of death for young people (the second most common cause for young men). The rate continues to rise—thirty-five per cent in the last ten years alone—as do the number of prevention programs and the amount of parental and community soul-searching. Yet a definitive answer to the tragic question of 'why' seems to elude us.

A sobering point in a far from sober book, yes, but a point that underlines my premise in a way that little else does. Great expectations can cripple our spirits and fuel despair. The greatest of them are heaped upon us at a time when we are at our most vulnerable—the precipice of adulthood.

Happiness, then, and survival too (of ourselves and the species), may well lie in taking a load off once in a while, having a good old laugh at the inevitabilities of what lies before us, and picking off life's too-great expectations one by one.

Life's too-great expectations

1 That fame = success = happiness

The belief that A-list famous people occupy a rarefied air of boundless money and all the trappings one needs to look perennially fabulous is what sees us purchase enough glossy magazines each week to keep Kerry Packer in new kidneys until the end of time.

The desire to be famous is now a given. And the proliferation of 'famous people' has made a life more ordinary than fame seem rather like death. You've got to be famous to be interesting; seen to be heard; noticed to be noted. To not be in the spotlight, especially now that talent and charisma are no longer prerequisites, is to be achingly mediocre and dull.

Even when we're shown the flipside of fame—the loss of privacy, the cruelty of critics, the resurrection of soft-porn flicks filmed at uni—the alternative seems worse: anonymity, boredom, bills, bosses, bunions.

Seldom do we think about the fickleness of fame, how quickly it all might end, how rough the grass might be at the end of that Slip-n-Slide. Reality TV especially, though making it infinitely simpler to sample a taste of notoriety, has effectively shortened fame's run from Warhol's promised fifteen minutes to about forty-five seconds. As acclaimed British photographer James Elliott put it recently: 'Fame divorced talent years ago and now just sleeps around with the media instead.' In turn, the media spits out famous people like old chewing gum: *You're hot, you're not, next*! Sadly, the trip back down from such giddy heights is seldom as quick or as fun as the trip up. It's like driving back from a great holiday with sunburn, five extra kilos and an empty wallet.

Never do we think about fame's bottom line cost—up to $70 million a year for all the requisite primping, preening and poncing, according to film industry bible *Variety*. Of course, garden-variety fame (following a stint on, say, *Big Brother* or *Australian Idol*) would cost considerably less to maintain, but then how do you put a price on all the jealous friends you'll lose in the process, the day-job you prematurely ditched, or the deep dark secret you had to sell to *New Idea* just to keep your flickering name up in lights?

And what makes you think you'd be any different from every other famous person who is patently miserable? Why wouldn't you too start thinking that your farts don't smell and that no-one and nothing is good enough for you, thus paving the way for a series of expensive divorces, burned critics, botched botox injections and a much-publicised stint or two in rehab? Why couldn't you slide from grace the same way, say, Whitney Houston did? When entering rehab in March 2004, Houston's spiritual advisor Prince Asiel Ben Israel said the celebrity lifestyle was directly to blame for Whitney's painful fall. 'When you've got the demands of the press and the public, you're trying to take a pill to stay up and a pill to lay down. It's that kind of life.' Similarly, one doubts

Mediocrity Hall of Fame

Life member: Adam Ant

Best known as a singer, albeit a crap one, Adam Ant (or Stuart Goddard as his mother knew him) has never been fairly credited for the pioneering efforts he made in the 1980s to turn music video clips into high-art. Brash, theatrical and unafraid of liquid blush, Ant's inherent mediocrity paved the way for fellow talentless types to have their fifteen minutes using fantastic film clips that take viewers' attention away from the banality and sheer badness of the actual music.

If not for such bravery, it could be argued, the music world would never have delivered Kylie Minogue, Peter Andre, the Spice Girls and boy bands en masse.

Michael Jackson is giggling his bleached head off behind all those face masks.

Yes, celebrity may well be the new currency, but who can afford the exchange rate? And why would you want to leave the couch anyway?

2   That hard work and sacrifice will necessarily lead to satisfying, well-paid work

In their thousands, decent hardworking Australians are fleeing their air-conditioned offices for the trackie-dacked sanctity of their home computers. Goodbye coffee rations, hello well-stocked pantry!

It's estimated that up to fifteen per cent of us now work from home, an increase of about five per cent in less than ten years. That's in spite of the fact that office jobs are still where the money is—Rolls Royces seldom emerge from customised sewing rooms strewn with Lego pieces and Barbie limbs—and in spite of the fact the average person needs infinitely more money to survive these days.

So what, aside from *Jerry Springer* re-runs and the freedom to pick one's nose mid-spreadsheet without being sprung, is fuelling this home-office revolution?

The answer of course is BOOFHEADS (Bosses Of Outrageously False Hubris Effected As Dickheadism).

Boofheads rule the world. They certainly rule an inordinate number of sections and divisions and departments and special projects at any rate. Cast your eye around any open-plan office and you will see, peering oafishly over their grey dividers, a boofhead plotting his or her next act of micro-managerial stupidity.

Some boofheads earn their places through years of well-timed boofheadish behaviour; others fall into management

Mediocrity Hall of Fame
Life member: Pete Best

'Dumped by The Beatles' is the mantle upon which drummer Pete Best has carved out what passes for a musical career. And by embracing the resultant mediocrity that was thrust upon him, Best has enjoyed an even longer career than his erstwhile companions.

The young musician had thought good looks alone would ensure his place alongside John, Paul and George back in 1961, but the Sideburned Ones thought differently. 'Pete had never been quite like the rest of us,' Paul McCartney has since said. 'We never really hung out together—he was slightly different.'

Ringo Starr, though, was nutty and fun-loving enough to fit right in. No better at drumming but tonnes more fun in the back of a van, Ringo quickly flicked Pete into musical obscurity.

More than forty years later, Pete (Bitter? Moi?) Best manages his own self-named band and has a website for fans that introduces him as 'The man who put the beat in Beatles' (not to be confused with 'The man The Beatles gave the boot').

positions and then become boofheads through a highly efficient process of osmosis. Still others are born into boofhead families and merely have to wait around until the kingpin of boofheads clutches his chest and falls to the shagpile.

Of course not all managers are boofheads, nor do all managers become boofheads, but the truth is undeniable: Australian workplaces are full of them. Official stats are hard to come by— the Australian Bureau of Statistics being oddly reluctant to commission a study with 'boofhead' in its title—but strong anecdotal evidence would suggest that approximately 68.47 per cent of managers and supervisors in Australia are definitely certifiable boofheads.

Most troubling about this situation is that boofheads don't appear to favour one industry over another. There aren't, for example, more boofheads in manufacturing than in the media (there simply couldn't be). So it's impossible to chart one's career path based on the desire to avoid boofheads. There does, however, seem to be a tendency to find more boofheads at the top of the corporate ladder than at the bottom—not unlike the way you'll often get the worst head of beer at the best hotel—which makes the appeal of jumping ship mid-career such a popular proposition these days.

What you'll have acquired by this stage of life, besides a basic skills set to take elsewhere, is the realistic awareness that no amount of hard work and sacrifice, and certainly no modicum of talent or initiative, will necessarily enable you to avoid or conquer the working world's many boofheads. Employment mediocrity, be it home-based, part-time, smart casual or via tele-commuting, could well be your only hope.

Because if corporate life's boofheads don't succeed in crushing your spirit, stealing your ideas, lashing you with paper cuts and drowning your soul in instant coffee, then it is only because you have become one yourself.

Go home. Think about it.

3 That the first cool mill. will be the hardest

Just as it's apparently easy to ignore the hoarse pleas of the starving and diseased in the world, it's simple to blank out the pained groans of the fabulously rich.

Rent-paying humans have long believed that the wealthy know something about pleasure that the rest of us don't; that money somehow diminishes our problems or at least buys more interesting ones, and we're not about to change our tunes anytime soon—at least not until we're fabulously rich enough to judge for ourselves.

Mediocrity Hall of Fame
Life member: Chevy Chase

America's best comedic actor or its worst judge of film scripts? Chevy Chase may well be remembered for the latter in the wake of a butchered career that seems too deliberate to be accidental.

For how does one explain the brilliance of *Caddyshack* in the context of what followed: *Oh Heavenly Dog!*, *Under the Rainbow*, *Deal of the Century*, *Spies Like Us*, *Nothing but Trouble*, *Memoirs of an Invisible Man*, *Cops and Robbersons* and a disastrous nightly TV talk show? Only *Fletch* and *National Lampoon's Vacation* have saved Chevy from becoming his own C-grade movie genre at the local video shop.

Given that he began his career as a brilliant writer of his own comedy scripts and cut his teeth among the best in the business via *Saturday Night Live*, it seems the only conclusion to draw is that Chase actively chose a future steeped in mediocrity rather than success.

This would also explain why Chase turned down the career-saving lead role in the Academy Award-blitzing *American Beauty*.

But perhaps he simply pursued the wrong career entirely. Few people know that Chase is blessed with perfect pitch and was once the drummer for a promising jazz band that went on to become Steely Dan.

Never mind that the obscenely wealthy English royal family is so rife with misery that the Queen only ever smiles at funerals. Never mind that forty per cent of the world's four hundred richest people describe themselves as being unhappy. Never mind that billionaire entrepreneurs like Rene Rivkin can't find an anti-depressant that's strong enough.

Never mind that a drug-addled Elvis Presley died sitting on the only seat in the house that could still hold his weight. Or that high-flying visionary Howard Hughes spent the last years of his life holed up in an air-conditioned chamber to prevent 'the flies from attacking'. The quest to be rich marches ever onward.

Yet so real is the disproportionate relationship between material wealth and personal satisfaction that psychologists have now identified the resultant, diagnosable malady and called it affluenza. Defined as 'a dysfunctional relationship with money or wealth and the pursuit of it', affluenza can strike down any rich bastard.

The 'sudden-wealth syndrome' is a scary prognosis. The key symptoms of affluenza—depression, addiction, guilt, broken relationships—are as easy to catch as sauce on a new tie. For the moneyed, they're harder to shake than a Rolexed real estate agent.

What starts out as a healthy type-A-personality-style pursuit of the material fruits of hard labour quickly morphs into a soul-destroying, rampant and ultimately empty devotion to money and materialism. Empty because, for all those long hours, burned friendships and shattered moral codes, there are still two things a stonkingly wealthy person can't avoid in life: death and . . . well, just death actually.

Affluenza is Samuel Johnson's troubling nineteenth-century prophecy writ large: 'Life is a progress from want to want, not from want to enjoyment.' Johnson rationalised that people don't get happier the more they own because our wants increase in proportion to our income.

Two centuries later, economist Richard Easterlin actually proved Johnson's theory correct. The 2003 results of his definitive twenty-eight-year study for the University of Southern California showed that people never actually get ahead of their material wants. They remain trapped on a hedonistic treadmill, effectively stuck in the same level of self-reported happiness they've always had.

Mediocrity Hall of Fame
Life member: Kevin Costner

It's a trifle ironic that Kevin Costner almost abandoned an acting career when the only early work he could get was in soft porn. Later, in 1999, he was only too happy to drop his towel for *The Love of the Game*, but reportedly test screen audiences were so doubled over by what they saw, or rather what they didn't see, that the nude scene was promptly deleted from the film.

At any rate, let's not be nasty. Kevin Costner makes the Hall of Fame firstly for single-handedly turning around a successful career with self-indulgent and just plain bad film projects (*Waterworld? The Postman? Message in a Bottle?* Hello? Hello? Hello?).

Secondly, his woeful acting isn't fooling anyone and it's no surprise Costner has won three Golden Raspberry Awards (1991, 1994 and 1997) as worst actor in a major film. These are the entertainment industry's alternative awards celebrating success through mediocrity.

Finally, in the category of plain old cluelessness, Costner gets the gong for converting the tract of land given to him by Sioux Indians after making *Dances with Wolves* into a golf course. Charmed, we're sure.

Money creates new problems and rarely solves old ones. I'm not making this up—it's scientific fact.

To counter this imbalance, Easterlin suggests that people actively convert the financial benefits of their higher productivity into increased leisure time and more satisfying family- and community-based endeavours. Only then, he says, can we hope to raise the bar of our personal happiness.

But that's where Easterlin gets a little ahead of himself methinks. That whole work hard/play hard philosophy can prove a real trap for the unwary, especially when you consider that it's

Mediocrity Hall of Fame
Life member: Graham Kennedy

When the 'King of Australian Television' hung up his crown in the late 1970s, no-one expected him to drop out of the limelight entirely. But for Kennedy, whose acerbic wit delivered Australia its first on-air 'F-word', a life not on the box might as well be in the box.

Kennedy traded success for a life so ordinary that his only communication with the outside world is via fax. Once mobbed and adored (but tellingly, with no-one to go home to at night), he chooses to spend his post-TV days on a remote property in the company of some Clydesdale horses, a dog and a few curious neighbours.

Reportedly, though, Kennedy hasn't lost his knack for the one-liner. When a neighbour used a tractor to bury Kennedy's favourite Clydesdale, Dave, the former star's golden retriever tried to dig up the carcass in the soft soil. 'Oh good', Kennedy mumbled to the tractor-owner, 'I'd like to see him again'.

just as easy to play hard without necessarily working too hard. Right, Hilton sisters? Even shopping is so much more fun when you just try on heaps of clothes and get thrown out of toffy-nosed boutiques than when you actually have to part with money.

If happiness does indeed come with a price tag, then why not let the rich and afflicted pay top dollar and wait instead for the markdowns? Everything goes on sale eventually.

Besides, you don't want to catch affluenza. It can really affect your sense of taste.

4 That you're no-one unless you own some real estate and then renovate it

I've given up trying to convince people that mortgages are about as sexy as belly-button lint, and that no-one bar big fat banks actually own anything. People don't *own*, they merely *owe*, and if that recognition gives you a warm feeling as you go to sleep each night, then I strongly suspect you've got the electric blanket up too high.

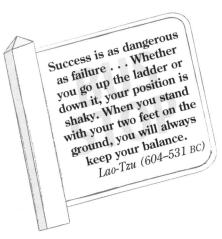

Success is as dangerous as failure . . . Whether you go up the ladder or down it, your position is shaky. When you stand with your two feet on the ground, you will always keep your balance.
Lao-Tzu (604–531 BC)

Yet the pressure to purchase real estate remains all-consuming. I'm not saying it's a bad move to make—hey, someone has to own the home I rent—but simply that it's not the essential rite-of-passage we've all been led to believe it is.

If being saddled with a thirty-year debt is your thing, if the millstone look works well for you, then by all means buy a home. But if you're not convinced that having a pathological fear of interest rate rises is a fun way to spend your thirties and forties, then don't be too quick to dismiss the mediocre joy of renting.

I love renting. I love the fact that when the ceiling falls in, or the hot water system bursts, or a hidden basement is discovered containing the bodies of the last eight tenants, then you just dial nine for Landlord. It's like an extended hotel stay—no pressure, just pleasure.

I especially love the fact that when it comes to all those miracle renovation programs on TV, I can watch them purely for the entertainment value. There is absolutely no pressure whatsoever to pick up a paintbrush and submit to the devil that is DIY. As a renter, I'm not even *allowed* to. It's incredibly liberating.

It is tempting, isn't it, to think that renovating might be a right spot of fun and paint-splattered hi-jinks when so many happy, good-looking folk seem to be doing it on TV. And when the only thing anyone discusses anymore at barbecues is the difference between how much they paid for their house and how much they expect to get at auction now that every second wall is a feature attraction.

Certainly, that was the conundrum my husband and I found ourselves in not so long ago when we realised that because we didn't own a home and wouldn't know a jigsaw if it came up and sanded us, we risked becoming pariahs—the sort of people you invite over once and once only. Never mind that we always brought along a lovely Mexican dip and more than our share of good wine to every social event. When it came to contributing to the latest round of banter on marble versus granite benchtops, we looked as lost as Lara Flynn Boyle in a pie shop.

Fortunately, though, we've gotten better at faking it. We now study up on the weekly plethora of lifestyle programs and real estate liftouts. We drive past auctions and open houses (and sometimes we don't even yell at the people inside to go home and stop checking out other people's cupboards). We peruse

Bunnings catalogues and eavesdrop on the heated conversations of the renovating couple over the back fence.

We are rent-paying phonies with some of the best made-up renovating anecdotes you've ever heard. Only our closest friends know that we won't actually be contributing a single brass razoo

Mediocrity Hall of Fame

Life member: Kylie Minogue

Many, many performers have ridden the road to pop glory armed with little more than a functioning voicebox and mountains of scrunchies, but none has been as successful, prolific or enduring as Australia's own Kylie Minogue.

'The singing budgie', as she was first known after sliding out from beneath Harold's jalopy on *Neighbours* and donning a bubble skirt, has proved all the naysayers wrong with a career that has spanned ten albums, oodles of awards and number one hits aplenty. Few would have predicted her hayfever-like tones would endure past breakfast, let alone spawn a greatest hits compilation. *I Should Be So Lucky* indeed.

A talent for reinvention, status as a gay icon, and a willingness to get her kit off in any sort of weather have collectively catapulted this pint-sized star into the modern legend stratosphere. Britain's loose interpretation of talent hasn't hurt either.

Dannii Minogue notwithstanding, few would begrudge Kylie her unprecedented level of mediocrity-derived success. And few know where or when her star may fade. Indeed, Kylie herself may be the only person who can jam a stick in her career's spokes, and she may well have done it recently when she declared she would no longer be baring her bum cheeks from here to breakfast.

Sweetie. It's not your high notes they clamour to see.

to the estimated \$6 *billion* that Australian couples and investors will spend on home renovations in the coming year.

We also won't be among the reported thirty-seven per cent of renovating couples for whom the process of taking on a 'fixer-upper' renders their marriage an irreconcilable broken-downer. (Truly, the figures are frightening.)

And we won't be party to the DIY craze that is sending the kids of unemployed tradesmen to school with empty lunchboxes and soleless shoes. (The only regular work most chippies and plumbers are getting these days is fixing the hatchet jobs of teachers and accountants and dentists who should have known better.)

And finally, we won't be losing any sleep over our responsibility for that bleak day in the future when people suddenly look around them and discover there isn't a single old kitchen left to replace in the whole world. That every front door has a stained glass insert, every floorboard is polished within an inch of its life, and every backyard has at least one water feature.

What then but the complete breakdown of society? Nothing to watch on TV, nothing to do on the weekends, nothing to budget for, nothing to fight over, nothing to read about, nothing to ponder, and nothing to bore others senseless with at barbecues.

Yes, it might not be cool to be a renting non-renovator at this juncture in time, but it's the least one can do for this great country of ours.

5 That there is someone for everyone

The genesis of this expectation is rooted in early childhood, when countless bedtime fairytales tell of star-crossed lovers, romantic paths ruled by destiny, and maiden after useless maiden being rescued by conveniently unattached princes in purple pantaloons. Further back still, the ancient Greeks engineered the philosophy of 'soulmates' with their myth about the origin of the two sexes. Apparently Zeus, king of the gods, owner of the power tools, wasn't happy with his initial creation of a single-sex creature that could reproduce without assistance and therefore wandered superciliously about the earth, needing nothing and wanting no-one. Zeus reportedly sent a lightning bolt down to split the creature in two, then sent all the half-creatures asunder so that it became virtually impossible—though compellingly irresistible—to spend one's life searching for our other half; for our one true soulmate.

The power of such mythology has reverberated through the ages, inspiring reams of serendipitous love songs, poetry, stories, movies and art. Sadly, though, it has also set up many unwitting young men and women for a painfully rude awakening: that while a princely kiss from one's destined true love is certainly desirable and unlikely to be knocked back, frankly any kiss will do in a pickle.

Yes, there *is* someone for everyone, but therein lies the problem. Someone can be *anyone*, anyone is *everyone*, so everyone's for everyone, potentially. Mr Right could also be Mr Not Quite Right, Mr Right On The Night, Mr Oh All *Right* Then or even just Mr Hey! Right On Time.

Subscribing to the belief that one has a soulmate who will somehow flag his or her arrival on the scene with presentation of the left baby bootie you lost all those years ago at the Agricultural Show is to outline the agenda for your first year in therapy. It's soul-destroying, misleading, and hopelessly grounded in untruth.

In my younger days working on newspapers, I interviewed an elderly couple who were celebrating their sixtieth wedding anniversary. 'What's the secret to keeping love alive all these years?' I asked them over tea and scones.

Mediocrity Hall of Fame
Life member: Sylvester Stallone

Sylvester Stallone has a crudely wielded set of forceps to thank for his career as one of Hollywood's highest paid actors. The doctor who brought him into the world caused baby Stallone's face to become partially paralysed on the bottom left-hand side, a condition that later manifested itself in a permanent sneer and a debilitating speech slur.

No matter. That's how Hollywood likes its monosyllabic action movie stars! As Stallone himself has said: 'The eyes droop, the mouth is crooked, the teeth aren't straight, the voice sounds like a mafioso pallbearer, but somehow it all works.'

Indeed it does work, quite in spite of the fact that the guy simply can't act. (Stallone now tops the list of performers whose acting efforts have earned them a Golden Raspberry Award. Sylvester has won an impressive nine Razzies and attracted twenty-nine nominations during the lengthy career he kicked off with porno flick *The Party At Kitty And Stud's*.)

Stallone's squillions and the underdog immortality of characters like Rocky Balboa have ensured Sylvester is having the last laugh against the schoolboys who once voted him 'Most likely to end up in an electric chair'.

The wiry gentleman replaced his teeth to answer my question. 'It's easy', he said. 'You pick one person, and you make it work.'

I marvelled at the simple genius of this philosophy.

Suddenly, the old woman jumped to her feet. 'I'm not your bloody slave!' she yelled, flinging jam and cream across the room.

'I don't mean *you*, you old fool', her husband replied. 'I mean the relationship—you make the *relationship* work.'

'Oh don't you go changing your story! You meant that you pick some poor sucker and you make her work. Make her get you this, make her get you that. Well, I'm not fetching one more thing for you *ever*! Understood?'

'Yes, well, I'll be off then,' I said, bundling up my notebook and handbag.

So anyway, I think some of the poignancy of that story gets lost in the detail. The gentleman's point—that love is not perfected in an instant but rather practised over the course of a lifetime—is one that made sense to me. And interestingly, it's one shared by many eminent psychologists.

So confident is Dr Robert Epstein, editor-in-chief of *Psychology Today*, that true love comes down to nothing more than basic compatibility and a reasonable stab of effort that he made himself the subject of a qualitative study designed to show that one can fall in love with pretty much anyone they're mildly attracted to, provided they make a conscious, serious and sustained attempt to learn to love them.

Over the course of four months, Epstein committed to exclusively dating a woman he hadn't previously known. They attended bi-weekly counselling sessions together that were designed to teach both parties how to trust, communicate, apologise, forgive and resolve their conflicts. Monitoring of the couple's growing love was via charts, scans, blood tests and personal accounts.

Epstein's study was reportedly an outstanding success. The couple fell in love. The second phase of the study, the sustenance and growth of that love, is still being assessed, but Epstein is confident. He told the UK's *Guardian* newspaper:

Romantic love has failed and dating is absurd. Our thinking on the whole issue of love has become utterly distorted. We need to choose someone with whom there is a basic compatibility and with whom we share some attraction.

A great many people with no love in their lives, or with many failures, could have lasting love within their grasp if they just went about it the right way. I've no doubt this will become a deep, permanent love.

So if it's true that we are all, in an innate Darwinian sense, destined to pursue love until our bits drop off, then dropping the expectation that there is someone for everyone, and accepting instead that everyone's up for a bit of someone, seems a frightfully healthy and fortuitously mediocre way to approach life don't you think.

Indeed, it resonates with my brother's sage advice for winning poker: 'Pick a card, any card. Play it close to your chest. Only cheat if you're prepared to be decked.'

Mediocrity Hall of Fame
Life member: Tiny Tim

For a man with a voice that caused cats to draft suicide notes and hair that looked like it was waiting for the right pasta sauce, Tiny Tim (aka Herbert Khaury) enjoyed a surprising amount of early showbusiness success. The world, it seemed, had been waiting for a weird guy with a ukulele.

Although originally a comedy act, Tiny Tim struck music gold with his quaint 1968 hit 'Tiptoe Through the Tulips'. Unfortunately, this led Tiny to believe that people liked him for his singing and not for the comic incongruity of a middle-aged man strumming a toy guitar. He released several more albums and conducted national tours.

But after the spectacle of his biggest performance—his live TV wedding to a young girl called 'Miss Vicky' watched by more than forty-five million viewers of Johnny Carson's *The Tonight Show*—Tiny Tim's star started to flicker. The fans moved on, his record contract was dropped and Miss Vicky asked for a divorce.

Still convinced of his own musical talent, however, Tiny Tim went on to record singles on small independent labels. His own mother wouldn't have found them if she'd worked part-time in a record shop. Then came his late-eighties' cassette-only release *The World's Longest Non-Stop Singing Record*, which he'd recorded live. Thankfully, it found a niche audience among FBI agents who reportedly still use it to break the spirit of hardened crime lords.

After self-destructing two marriages, Tiny Tim drifted into a psychological abyss. He took to wearing adult diapers and baggy women's underwear. He spent his life in tawdry hotel rooms, funded by pathetic comeback attempts in small clubs.

But blessedly, the entertainment world's most tragic clown died doing what he thought people loved best—singing. He had a heart attack while tiptoeing through the tulips at a small concert in Iowa.

6 That two kids will do nicely thanks

For all the vast differences in human dreams and ambitions, the most basic plan is this: get a job, get married, have kids. The rest is so much window dressing.

Yet only two of these goals are readily achievable by everyone—namely, gainful employment and marriage. Any wingnut can find a job if they really want one, and, as discussed in the previous section, when it comes to finding a person willing to attend to your back pimples for the foreseeable future, there are plenty of someones for everyone.

Procreation—on paper, the simplest and perhaps most enjoyable part of the three-point life plan—is actually the most difficult and least likely event to successfully occur.

According to the latest statistics, a staggering one in six Australian couples are considered infertile (by definition: unable to conceive a child after at least twelve months of actively trying). This sad eventuality leads many of them down the path to IVF, itself a twenty per cent hit-and-miss proposition, and many many more down the road to Splitsville.

The discovery that one or both parties can't seem to pull off the most fundamental and apparently natural act befitting of humankind is a shattering realisation. It's made worse when all about you couples seem to be having children with gay abandon. Are they more worthy than you? Do they know something you don't? How can they see for all that smugness?

Nothing prepares you for the possibility that baby-making just might not happen for you. That you might never experience the miracle of birth. Never hear the pitter-patter of tiny feet not belonging to mice beneath your floorboards. All those life skills classes back in school taught you were how babies were *made*.

Not how they *weren't* made. Not how they could be comprehensively botched along the short journey from boozy dinner to sweaty brow. The likelihood of at least one lousy sperm out of every few million not reaching such a fish-in-the-barrel target seemed, well, inconceivable.

And then of course, for those clever types who do manage to pull off conception immaculately, there's the all-too rarely discussed but increasingly likely possibility of miscarriage to contend with. It's a fact that a whopping twenty-five to thirty per cent of all pregnancies end in miscarriage—a figure that has steadily risen with both the increased use of hormone-based contraceptives in recent decades and the dietary proliferation of Chicken-With-Mood-Swings Tonight.

Of course, you won't hear such conclusions drawn by doctors, but then doctors haven't even got their heads around the fact that miscarrying couples actually lose a baby, and not simply last week's Lotto entry. Even the term miscarriage sounds like

Mediocrity Hall of Fame

Member: Alicia

The most listened-to pre-teen in world history? That would be Alicia, the Scottish schoolgirl who became the youngest ever person to record the voice for the Speaking Clock. Although her parents were initially wary about letting their twelve-year-old say 'At the third stroke…' to eighty million complete strangers each year, they were impressed that she would achieve more exposure than Britney Spears without even having to bare her midriff.

a dodgy train ride and nothing at all like the tragic, abrupt and heartbreaking death that it is.

In light of the many hundreds of things that can go wrong between actively trying for a child and wiping the goo off a newborn, conception alone should be considered a remarkable achievement—a feat worthy of community accolades. Just because two drunk teenagers can pull it off behind an amenities block in the dark shouldn't make it any less awe-inspiring.

But while enough lucky people do continue to have babies— many of them at later and later intervals to allow for pressing engagements like having a life—and while sex education classes continue to stall at that hilarious moment when the teacher pulls a prophylactic over the head of a limp banana, then I doubt we'll see conception attracting the reverence it deserves.

It shall remain, like finding a job and getting hitched, this thing that you'll inevitably *do* when you're good and ready. A misleadingly simple expectation hiding a wealth of possibilities, good and bad.

Make no mistake, though. Creating new people is a big fat hairy deal. God may well have given us the tools, but the assembly instructions might as well be from IKEA.

7 That friendship is forever

'Friends aren't necessarily the people you like best. They are merely the people who got there first.' So said Peter Ustinov, categorically ditching his chances of a job at Hallmark Greeting Cards. Yet I'm inclined to agree with the furry philosopher.

Friendship has long been held aloft as a saviour of the human spirit, a filler of the voids left by loneliness and marriage, yet in reality much of its reputation is built on sentiment more than sincerity. The sandpit promises of kindergarten—'Let's be friends forever and ever!'—establish an early belief in the enduring power of friendship; in the serendipitous wonder of meeting someone who makes you laugh and learn and feel and experience more than you'd ever be able to on your own.

But then somehow friendship gets swamped, replaced by life and change and responsibilities and circumstance. And often, by friendship itself.

We know that this happens. We look back through our high school yearbooks, through our many office farewell cards, through Christmas cards stuffed with photos and letters, and we see a library of unfulfilled promises to stay in touch, to never grow apart, to be friends forever and ever. Yet we keep on making promises, we keep on believing in the dream, until slowly, inevitably, we move on to rationalisations, lame excuses and, finally, shameful ducking and weaving acts in the supermarket.

Why can't we openly acknowledge when a friendship has run its course? Why can't we say 'Look, it's been great, but I think we're going to have to call it a day because of [new job, move interstate, your decision to sleep with my wife]'? Why this charade about always catching up?

I know people who make it their second full-time job to catch up with old friends. It is both inspiring and utterly exhausting to behold. The trouble with their efforts is that they can only ever be one-dimensional and ultimately shallow—no-one can maintain deep and abiding friendships with the four thousand people they've met since Finger-painting 101.

Certainly, though, the advent of email has given them licence to try. The group email is the dodgy chain letter of my youth: a ten-for-the-price-of-one bulk catch-up deal, usually with a bonus guilt trip tacked on to the end. 'You've been tagged by the Hug Bear—pass it on!' 'Save a limbless child in Nantucket by

forwarding this message onto fifteen people in fifteen seconds.'
And of course those inane pop quizzes about what your favourite
colour of ice-cream is and what you happen to be wearing at this
pivotal juncture in history. 'How well do you really know your
friends? Fill in this quick quiz and pass it on. It's fun!'

I never forward any of these emails, mainly because I don't
know how to properly spell 'AaaarrrrGGGGGHHH!'. Nor do I know
how to begin to question the motives of friends who no doubt
mean well but who, in all other respects, seem too intelligent to
challenge the notions of free will and original thought.

But you know what? They still keep coming anyway.

It would probably be so much easier and less stressful to
simply pass them along, play the game, turn the other cheek and
let go of my angst. But I'm too far gone for that. In fact, if I see
one more angel bear flying about my computer screen and faffing
on about the true meaning of friendship while 'That's What
Friends Are For' wafts softly in the background, I swear I'll rip off
its cyber wings and pummel them with my mouse.

If email, as social commentators attest, has made the world
smaller and all of its inhabitants closer, then why do I feel so
ostracised when the best most friends can manage these days
is a group email written by someone else entirely? If a mass-
produced greeting card warrants a personalised message inside,
then why doesn't an email?

And why, it should be asked, has the reputation of friendship
survived in the face of so many outright betrayals by so-called
friends? Human beings are conditioned to hurt those closest to
them and the access and emotional exposure afforded by friendship makes this exceedingly possible. A friend may well be the
person at your side when life goes to hell in a handbasket, but
therein may lie the problem.

Cynical, yes, but I've been burned and I bet you have too. Would we have been so vulnerable if we didn't believe in the sandpit-derived sanctity of unending friendship? Would we have laid bare our deepest, darkest secrets if we thought they'd go on to become hilariously embellished anecdotes for a party of ten? Would we have exposed our Achilles heel if we looked upon friendship as an agreement without rules, without a contract, without an escape clause?

Finally, if we know how much we ourselves have the capacity to hurt others, then why don't we rightly expect friends to be capable of the same?

The answer, my friend-in-passing, is that we are taught to expect greater things of friendship. We are sold fairytales, we are softened by the innocence of children, we are seduced by *Thelma and Louise* and *Butch Cassidy and the Sundance Kid*—and look how things ended for them, huh?—and we are even conned by the empty promises we make ourselves.

A far more rewarding, albeit safe and mediocre, approach to friendship is to treat it as one does a favourite restaurant: sensational at its best, worthy of support, and hopefully here for the long haul. But resist the temptation to pledge unconditional patronage—even the best restaurants can go buffet overnight.

8 That when all else fails, you'll always have your parents

No wonder our parents seem better adjusted than us. For most of them, life's big safety net was still intact: the original family home. When the going got tough, the tough got going to Mum's—the one homefire that would always burn.

Our parents' parents' nest, though empty of children, was still full of memories, traditions, faded linen, chipped crockery and usually two folk driven to pickling all of the above in a rich family preserve. Even the old bedrooms remained in their virginal state—with *Charlie Brown* comics on the overhead bookcase, kewpie dolls on the patchwork eiderdown, and a leather switch still swinging on the back of the door.

Speaking generally, retirement for the 'traditionalist' generation born between 1900 and 1945 was about enjoying some hard-earned downtime after a working life defined by self-discipline and the motivation to benefit their children through major sacrifices. That enjoyment came through doting on the grandkids, throwing large family dinners, handsewing heirlooms and generally shuffling about in their house of memories until the nursing home or a spare room somewhere beckoned. The pension more than paid for such modest luxuries.

The traditionalists' children, our parents, the so-called baby-boomers, were less altruistic in their outlook. Their generation was the first to ask 'What about me?' They indulged a more optimistic passage of history with rank individualism, self-forged career opportunities, minimal sacrifice, and life plans drafted on Magnadoodles.

Perhaps necessarily, thanks to the economic effects of a now ageing population, baby-boomers are similarly approaching retirement with an attitude of self-reliance and 'What's in it for me?' They're deferring the end of work, not only because there's no way they can fund the lifestyle they desire on a measly pension and a drip-feed super fund, but also because they don't want to give up the means of self-expression and the personal sense of challenge that working represents.

That is why today's empty nest really is empty. Barren. Void. Mum and Dad are out working, learning, retraining, rebuilding, rethinking and rediscovering their inner rebels. They're divorcing each other, having their roots done, investing in apartments and

Mediocrity Hall of Fame
Life member: David Hasselhoff

'Beyond its entertainment value, *Baywatch* has enriched and, in many ways, helped save lives.'

Perhaps David Hasselhoff was referring to the time when the sight of Pamela Anderson's left breast escaping out of her red cossie caused my husband to wrest himself out of a beer-induced coma. At any rate, the man who came to prominence as Snapper in *Young and the Restless* has always believed in his ability to turn crap into cream.

And why not? At best an average actor and a karaoke-worthy singer, Hasselhoff has nevertheless become one of the most recognised faces on international television and a massive recording star in Germany. On the latter front, he's released nine successful albums for Teutonic groovers and his 1989 hit single, 'Looking for Freedom', remained number one there for eight consecutive weeks.

Unfortunately, US chart success has eluded Hasselhoff. His last attempt to crack American audiences was by way of a live pay-per-view concert from Atlantic City, but the sight of O.J. Simpson hurtling down an LA freeway in a white Bronco at exactly the same moment proved too tempting for most viewers. Thankfully, plenty of *Baywatch* scripts called for Mitch Buchanan to rescue dull days at the beach with impromptu singing displays.

Hasselhoff's gift for transcending talent is a marvel to behold. When his first incarnation of *Baywatch* was axed after just one season, Hasselhoff took implants into his own hands by self-financing the resurrection of the series. With plotlines thinner than a g-string and actors who missed out on callbacks for soft-drink commercials, the series went from strength to strength, winning more than one billion weekly viewers across one hundred and forty countries at the height of its popularity. Spin-off series shot up like unwanted ground cover and sold for millions of dollars each.

Success through mediocrity...David Hasselhoff, take a bow.

finding new loves (within a few years, they'll officially have the best odds of any Australian age group of picking up on a Friday night—it's true!).

Which is all well and good—who'd deny them?—but what about their kids, the Generation X-ers? What happened to their Sunday roast? Their crocheted blankets? Their fireside chats about the good old days? What happened to their old bedrooms? Their sense of the rich tapestry that weaves itself through family generations?

When Generation X-ers look back to the home they grew up in for hints on how their adult lives should take shape, what do they see? They see *units*! They see the redeveloped site where their family home once stood. History has been bulldozed. Raped by progress; cut down by the ambition of a generation who dared to see a life beyond kids.

The traditional expectation that when all else fails, one's parents will always be there to pay the bail money has not kept pace with the changing face of retirement in this country. The over-sixties aren't stopping. They're just getting started.

Don't just settle for second best. Grab it with both hands.

Chapter 3

The essentially ordinary guide to health, wealth and wisdom

Success is getting what you want. Happiness is wanting what you get.
Dostoyevsky, (1821–81)

Mediocrity is keeping both options open. Indefinitely.
Carrie Cox (1972–)

Healthy, wealthy and wise. Like Shane Warne, mobile coverage and trouble, these three always seem to be found together. But are they truly synonymous or merely the construed product of a little rhyming and alliteration? Can wealth buy health? Do wise people necessarily make healthy decisions? Does intelligence attract success? Does a one-legged duck swim in circles?

This alleged triumvirate of goodness could well be an axis of evil. A trap for the unwary. It could even simply be a convenient way of tying together an otherwise dog's breakfast of a chapter.

May the farce be with you

The trouble with pursuing good health is that it's a complete waste of time. Not just because you're going to die anyway and probably within choking distance of a rowing machine, but mainly because humans just aren't smart enough to nail health once and for all.

Mediocrity Hall of Fame
Member: Shane Warne

It's difficult to comprehend how someone as naturally talented as Australia's greatest ever leg-spin bowler can be so apparently hellbent on being remembered for anything but. Yet bamboozling people has always been one of Shane Warne's special talents.

In 1998, Warnie might have been able to blame youthful naivety for his part in accepting money from an Indian bookmaker in exchange for information about match reports and weather conditions, but it seems he learnt little from the resultant $8000 fine and public humiliation. Not long after, he was caught smoking while being paid as an advocate of Nicorette, the maker of anti-smoking patches. In fact, like an errant schoolboy, he was busted several times, once by two young fans to whom he promptly directed a crude earful.

While on tour in England, the married father engaged in phone sex with an English nurse. Golly, who'd have thought she'd run to the media with her sordid tale?! The indiscretion, for which he apologised, as in 'I'm so sorry I got caught', cost him the vice-captaincy of the Australian cricket side, a stain he may never erase.

But wait, there's more! In early 2003, Warne returned a positive drug test during the Aussie team's preparation for the World Cup. Shocked and desperately pleading his innocence, Warne later admitted he did take a banned substance—a diuretic that treats blood pressure, causes rapid weight loss and, uh-oh, can be used to mask steroid use—but only because his mother told him too. Silly old *Mum*.

Banned from playing representative cricket for a year, Shane was soon back to his sexually accident-prone best. In August 2003, a

South African woman accused Warne of harassing her with explicit text messages after a close encounter. Although Shane and his defenders maintain the claims were spurious and nothing more than a blatant attempt to extort money, they unearthed a rash of similarly sordid claims, including the revelation from a Melbourne lap-dancer that she'd had a three-month affair with the cricketer.

Too much fame too early? Too many women? Too much money and spare time? One thing's for certain: Shane Warne risks being remembered not as one of the nation's finest ever cricket players, but as one of its dumbest blonds.

The world of health research is as dodgy as my accountant. No sooner have the collective laboratory dorks spouted yet another 'essential', life-prolonging, waist-whittling behaviour than suddenly they scream 'No! Wait! Forget everything we said, okay?' And a new round of completely contradictory advice soon follows.

Among the latest revelations are that walking is actually bad for you (far better to aqua-plane?) and that beer is better in large quantities than small (my father may well live to see his 400s). And never mind that for the last five years we've all been drinking an aquarium-ful of water each day. Scientists now say the only benefit all that water is offering is the amount of exercise we're getting by bolting to the toilet every half-hour.

As for gingko biloba—that miracle product you've been taking for the last two years to ward off dementia—turns out it does about as much for your short-term memory as a case of Bundaberg Rum. In fact scientists have found it to be *less* effective than placebo, much to the chagrin of the mega-bucks industry that's flourished around it.

A quick word here in defence of the placebo. How did this intrinsically harmless entity become the benckmark for ineffectiveness? When so many things in life do more harm than good, how did something that does nothing at all get to have such a bad name? As entertaining medical commentator Dr Andrew Saul points out, the great majority of our illnesses are in fact self-limiting. About eighty per cent of sick people will either get better or die, regardless of what their doctor does. Saul argues that in all the studies where a placebo is used as a comparative measure, the good money should be on the placebo. They're safer, cheaper and often—perplexingly—more effective. He also cites that in the nineteenth century, a placebo 'movement' developed among doctors; physicians who no longer believed in artificial quick fixes started dispensing only placebos. Incredibly, their cure rate was higher and their death rate lower than previously, although of course you won't read about their groundbreaking work in today's fat medical tomes.

The simple fact is, it would seem, that often it pays to do nothing at all to achieve some good. Time, as they say, heals most wounds, and those that don't heal with time aren't going to heal at all. For all the money and hope we've thrown at cancer research over the years, the five-year survival rates for the most fatal breeds have not changed for the past fifty years. And the only solutions we've been able to throw at heart disease are more time on the treadmill and fewer two-for-one pizza deals.

So multi-billion-dollar medical industry notwithstanding, placebos can't be such a bad thing and they should, in fairness, have their reputation for 'first doing no harm' fully restored. What you don't know doesn't work, can't hurt you.

Moving on. It's to food that scientists particularly flock. Like mozzies to a Sunday picnic, they hover about our shopping trolleys, our pantries, our freezers and our bathroom scales, theorising and dictating to their scientific hearts' content, constantly coming up with new and entirely contradictory ways to mess with our heads and question every morsel of food we pop into our hungry mouths.

Yes, it's true that the diet industry is where the big research bucks are and even scientists' kids need new school shoes now and then. And, yes, it's true that we're a collectively overweight nation with more McDonald's outlets than churches. But at what cost our sanity? At what price the right to buy a loaf of bread without our heads imploding?

I was confused enough trying to follow the low-carbs theory on healthy eating (now so two months ago). Suddenly a salad sandwich was not the safe lunch option I'd always thought it to be, at least not while it involved two slices of demonically possessed bread. And what of rice, the staple diet of the world's thinnest nations? Granulated evil in disguise?

Still, if Jennifer Aniston could forego her penne boscaiola just to nab Brad Pitt with a pert bod (even if it ultimately became for nought), I too could curb my carbolic ways. Or so I thought. Darn it if I didn't get so hungry that I ended up eating my *Low-carbs diet book* on a giant French stick with a tortellini side dish. And darn it if I didn't also lose my mind just prior to throwing in the KFC mini handtowel.

See, what the low-carbs folk don't tell you about carbs is that they are the bridge pylons for your sanity. Without them, your brain quickly turns to roadbase and your emotional intelligence

dips to amoeba level. Ladies, if you thought (or more likely your partner *alleged*) that PMT made you crazy, you ain't seen or hurled nothing yet. The low-carbs diet will have all around you reaching for pillows with which to smother themselves. Meanwhile, you'll be standing on the bathroom scales shouting to the world that you've lost two kilos, haven't eaten wheat in three weeks and would very much like to impale your flatmate on a fondue stick. Trust me, the next time you meet a cranky person, just stuff a sandwich in their gob and wait for the hugs to start.

More recently, it's GI that has fashion-savvy nutritionists in a tizz. GI (as in 'Gee I think it's time we gave the fatties something new to obsess about') focuses on a food's glucose content and, in turn, the rate at which it breaks down in the body. The theory, pinched from the realm of diabetes where, okay, it does have sound and important applications, is that low-GI foods are better for us because they break down more slowly in the body and leave us feeling less hungry afterwards. Scientifically, this may well be true, but if you're anything like me, you do *not* want to be waiting around all afternoon for your lunch to digest just so that you can enjoy your mid-afternoon Mars bar with a strawberry milkshake chaser. Life's short, let's keep the food chain moving, peoples!

So popular is this new theory that a packaging symbol has been created to make it easier to 'shop smarter'. I don't know about you, but smart shopping for me is any grocery excursion that doesn't involve losing my child in the fruit-n-veg section or forgetting four out of the five items I originally popped out for. As for checking every label for its GI content, I've got the time if you've got next year's Melbourne Cup winner.

At any rate, the GI diet is like so many other scientific theories that seek to personalise food into good guys and bad guys. But what did a choc-chip muffin ever do to hurt anybody? When was the last time bread insulted your mother?

Until particular food stuffs start threatening us directly, I say we shouldn't be declaring war on them, not even when scientists tell us they're carb-loaded, oligopoly-saturated, fat-magnetised, cholesterol-charged and that the GI ratings are off the charts and climbing. If one waits around long enough, every dietary habit will have its month in the sun, drunken binges and chiko rolls included.

Best stick, then, to those basic tenets of health that don't require scientific justification: namely, that putting something edible in your mouth several times a day appears to ensure survival, that KFC is the only sure cure for a hangover, and that the only thing guaranteed not to hurt is a good lie-down.

In many ways, the lie-down is the flipside of the placebo effect. Whereas the placebo effect involves something that seems like it's-doing good but is actually doing nothing, rest feels like it's doing nothing when it's actually doing a whole lot of good.

These days we scoff at doctors who prescribe rest, feeling as though we haven't got our $45-per-consultation worth. The simple fact is they're probably prescribing us the most effective elixir of all.

So why do we find it hard to just simply rest? Why is a good lie-down harder to come by than a well-aligned shopping trolley? It can't simply be that we're so much busier now, although that's arguably true. There must be something more diabolical at work here; something that has successfully turned the humble rest into an object of scorn and shame.

If you've got time for a rest, the thinking now goes, there must be something important you're not doing; some 30-minute daily walk you're not taking or twelfth glass of water you're not drinking. A rest is nothing if it's not value-added with a yoga pose and a chant. Indeed, a rest on its own is simply lazy. Not therapeutic. Not biologically essential. Just lazy.

Well, I blame the self-help movement for this one. It should be shot.

If our thinking doesn't change, if a daily rest isn't restored to its rightful position on the medical tree of remedies, then I predict we face a bleak future of endless colds, super-flus and general malaise. Tiredness will become the new black; cough medicine the new multi-vitamin, taken daily.

As cartoonist Michael Leunig's Mr Curly says, 'It is worth doing nothing and having a rest, in spite of the difficulty it may cause you'.

It's just possible a decent lie-down might be all the cure we're looking for.

What's to work out? Exercise sucks

People who know me will allege that I'm not qualified to write about exercise because I've never once set foot inside a gymnasium.

But there's a very good reason for that. I happen to have an inbuilt radar for con jobs and I've never found any more cunning than the gym.

For three decades, I have watched and wept as countless friends and relatives have marched determinedly through the double-glass doors of some flash new facility, only to return beaten, bruised and burnt by rash lycra purchases. I have silently mocked their many sorry tales told of wasted annual memberships, overcrowded saunas, long waits for the treadmills and, perhaps most disturbing of all, exercise *addictions* (puh-lease). I have listened and I have learned and I have decided over and over: there but for the grace of God go I. Put one foot in and they'll want me to shake it all about.

Gyms may well have started out with good intentions—healthy body, healthy mind, blah, blah, blah—but they've become horribly evil over the years. Once was the time a fitness class meant aerobics, and it came in three styles: beginners, intermediate and advanced. Beginners classes were for hopeful fatties, advanced classes were for eager first-timers hopelessly overshooting the mark, and intermediate classes were empty. Now there are more types of classes than there are body parts for piercing. It seems the same Unnecessary Complication Virus that has infected sports shoes, pubs and the humble cup of coffee has had its dastardly way with gyms.

The basic fitness class 'menu' now reads like a how-to guide for mastering the tango: Step, Box, Twist, Resist, Double-Step, Pump, Squat, Burn, Turn, Grimace Broadly. Worse are the hybrid creations, clearly named by instructors on some form of macrobiotic smack: Boxercise, Step-Pump Attack, Combat Resista-twist, Cycle-robics and Aqua-everything. And can there really be sleep lost over Yogalates versus Piloga?

Oh I see what the thinking is here: variety equals value equals more members. It's Marketing 101. But in a world where everything is already too damn hard, what's the sense in applying 248 names to what basically amounts to an hour of star jumps? And why make any harder something that already hurts like buggery?

Given the difficulty level in simply finding something to wear to the gym (and don't give me that 'A t-shirt and shorts will be fine' line—you KNOW who they'll be laughing at when you roll up in anything less than a shiny bra and reflective tights!), you'd think gyms would be making it easier, not harder, to decipher the products and services they have on offer. You'd think they'd call every class Exercise and every circuit Machine Stuff. You'd think each piece of equipment would include a 'How To Get The Hell Off' advice sticker and an emergency Allen key. You'd think they'd give your brain a rest while they sap your body of life. But no.

Of course one could hire a personal trainer to make sense of all this palaver, but what can be right about exercising in front of a person who already has a butt that could crack eggs and a look that says 'And you should see me *without* my clothes on'. I'm sorry but that's about as appealing as double dating with Angelina Jolie.

It's one thing to want to lose some weight when approaching fatty-boombah status, but it's entirely another to buy into the modern gym philosophy of changing everything about yourself bar the correct attachment of limbs. I have several slim, healthy and otherwise sensible friends who run half-marathons on the treadmill each day just to lose their cellulite. Here's the thing . . . *even* babies have cellulite. It's not going anywhere because it's meant to be there. Don't ask me why; it just is. And if you're really so concerned about changing your apparently

Mediocrity Hall of Fame
Member: Zhang Di

In 2004 twenty-six-year-old Zhang Di became the first woman to win China's Miss Ugly contest, the forerunner to its hosting of the Miss World competition. Nudging out fifty other hopefuls, each vying to be judged the woman most in need of plastic surgery, Zhang won a $16 500 gift voucher for facial reconstruction—enough, the contest's sponsor assured, to make her 'a totally different girl' within weeks.

Perhaps she should save it for therapy.

Still, at least Zhang has something to live for. In a society that now rates extreme makeovers more highly than uni degrees, being deemed ugly gives one an exciting and potentially limitless scope for reinvention. On the other hand, your Linda Evangelista types really have nowhere to go—no surgeons to visit on a Saturday night, no reality TV shows to sell their soul to, no 'before' and 'after' shots to wow the crowds with. Indeed, the only way they earn magazine covers these days are through bad hair days, sans-make-up trips to the shops, and cellulite-ridden romps along the beach.

hideous backsides, why don't you—I don't know—*stop buying g-strings*?

Truly, it's as silly as men who'll do and pay anything to hide their encroaching baldness. Most women like male baldness—some of us even find it dead-sexy—in the same way that most men would opt for a size-14 woman over a size-10 bonebag any day of the week. I particularly don't understand why men would do anything but welcome the opportunity to eliminate hair maintenance from their lives once and for all. If women could eliminate hair maintenance, they'd be running the armed forces and commanding media empires in between scone bake-offs. We've got the talent; we just don't have the time. The glass ceiling is rendered with styling products.

But back to fitness. No actually, enough of that. I'm about to cough up a lung. Let's just leave it that gymnasiums have unnecessarily complicated the field of health and you'd do well to stay away from them. Resist those cries of 'Come over here fatty!', resist the lure of 'Never-to-be-repeated-until-next-month' membership deals, and instead head to the nearest DVD store and ask for the 'Family Popcorn Movie Special'. It's low-fat, it's cheap and no-one cares if your g-string rides above your trackie-daks.

I am woman, hear me snore!

Statistically, women are physically healthier specimens than men. They live longer, and generally when they look like they might be eight months' pregnant, it is a baby not a weekly slab of beer.

Ironically, though, it's the pressure women put on themselves to look healthier (read: thinner) that sees them fall behind men in the mental health stakes. Women are hopeless slaves to the glossy whims of magazines, forever comparing themselves to airbrushed ideals and pampered celebrities. They fear ordinary and drive themselves mad in their quest to change every single aspect of that which nature dished up. Men look at George Clooney, shrug, and order pizza.

Interestingly, many of the so-called beautiful people who women idolise in their quests to change everything about

themselves are no happier than your average housewife. In fact, some are downright depressed, disturbed and damaged by the omnipresent pressure to look good, live well and eat rarely. Why else is Claudia Schiffer thin enough to court bolognaise? Why is Cindy Crawford constantly racked by reports of her husband's cheating? Why do Kate Moss and Naomi Campbell get so nervous around airport sniffer dogs? It seems likely the only uber-gorgeous celebrities who seem genuinely happy have had their smiles painted on by the *Women's Weekly* Airbrushing Department.

Perhaps if female celebrities themselves revolted against the pressure to be ever thinner and younger, the average ordinary woman would follow suit.

On that score, it was recently encouraging to see Elle Macpherson, one of Australia's wealthiest and arguably healthiest-looking women, fling her g-string back at the industry that made her a supermodel, declaring that the media pressure for post-baby slimness was just too great. 'It's like there's this competition; who can lose the weight quickest after a baby. It's unhealthy', she told *Harper's Bazaar* (essential reading for every woman up to her elbows in Napisan). While she'll still be hawking her doily-sized knickers and bras from here to breakfast (and can finally breathe out, amen), the body known as The Body has decided to leave the rampant flashing to a younger crop of models. Even she, the nation's paragon of anatomical perfection, seems aware that the fight against gravity is all for nought, and that at the end of the day the only thing more inevitable than stretchmarks after childbirth is butt-sag after thirty.

Many women have always known this, having watched our mothers struggle through Jane Fonda workouts only to end up hurling the video case at the TV when it was discovered Jane didn't mind a dash of collagen with her star jumps thanks very much. But one wonders what tipped Elle over. Was it the 2 a.m. toilet visits—those pressing nightly reminders that a once robust bladder has gone to the dogs? Was it the first time she discovered that the skin under her arm keeps waving goodbye long after the hand has finished? Was it the flamenco-style clicking of her hip joints upon getting into and out of the car? Did she fall asleep on a rough piece of carpet and find the imprint on her face for the next week?

No, it is probably far more likely that Elle Macpherson, like so many other busy women and working mums these days, is simply *stuffed*. The latest international figures have revealed that a staggering eighty-two per cent of working mums (like there's any other kind) survive on less than five hours' sleep each night. About forty per cent would be classified as clinically depressed if, Prozac willing, they had the time to be diagnosed. While good make-up does much to hide the modern working mum's resultant 'dazed and confused' look, the fact remains that most of them are stumbling about from family crisis to committee meeting on little more than a cup of strong coffee and a sloppy 6 a.m. kiss from a three-year-old. That they command vehicles in supermarket carparks is frankly terrifying.

Men simply don't let themselves get as rundown and exhausted as women do. Wisely, they allow themselves to concentrate on one thing at a time and consequently do that thing relatively well. They relax without letting themselves feel guilty about it. They don't trouble themselves about remembering family birthdays and key events. They don't worry about neglecting their friends. They trust that women will do enough worrying about the state of their relationship for both of them. They watch whole TV shows. They sleep eight hours a night. Their hair doesn't move.

Women would do well to follow men's lead (or lack thereof) in this arena. They should ignore the ghosts of pioneering feminists baying at their heels. For all that bra-burning achieved, the reality is that modern women have gone and whipped themselves into vicious circles of exhaustion, the high price of which is exacted in their health, their self-esteem and their relationships.

Women need to stop this madness. They need to listen to men when they say, remote in hand, 'Sit down already! The footy's about to start'. They need to move the goalposts (preferably closer to the clubhouse) and change all the rules of this mad game called daily life. They need to scream: 'I am woman! Hear me snore! I can't keep running anymore!'

Where there's smoke, there's dumbness

While we're on health matters, I feel compelled to touch briefly upon the issue of smoking. I'm sorry, but it is one of the *dumbest* things a person can do. Not mediocre, not even ordinary, just dumb. Smoking claims more human lives daily than text-messaging drivers, yet no amount of rotting lung pictures will curb their ways.

The answer, for the sake of the human race, is to sack all the BMW-driving ad people paid to conjure images of fetid body organs and instead fork out a far more mediocre sum to an advertising campaign that embraces the more subtle side of ordinary. Behold a new generation of cigarette-packet wake-up calls:

WARNING: Smoking produces unsightly rectangular shirt bulges in your shirt pockets and trousers.

WARNING: Smoking outside buildings makes you a captive audience for street sellers, religious zealots and bums wanting money (for cigarettes).

WARNING: Smoking seriously limits your first-impression prospects with potential in-laws, even, strangely enough, if they happen to be smokers themselves.

WARNING: Smoking makes you look like an addict. And seriously, that's about as attractive as socks with sandals.

WARNING: Smoking will hinder your career prospects, mainly because your non-smoking workmates don't actually appreciate picking up the slack caused by your frequent twenty-minute disappearing acts. Sometimes they even call you 'the fat lazy bastard downstairs again'.

WARNING: All smokers cough like old men sleeping in bus shelters.

WARNING: Smoking causes you to assume permanent awkward hand poses and finger gestures, with or without cigarettes within striking distance.

WARNING: You do smell bad. No, really. You reek.

WARNING: Smoking makes you the enemy of large blokes called firemen.

WARNING: 19 000 people like you died of a smoking-related disease last year. Oh, but you're DIFFERENT, aren't you?

WARNING: What are we going to say at your funeral? That you went before your time? That your death came as a terrible shock to us all? HA! Bring on the 'I told you so's'!!!

A job by any other name

I have long been of the opinion that if work were such a splendid thing, the rich would have kept more of it for themselves.

Bruce Grocott (1940–), *The London Observer*, 1988

It's a rude awakening indeed to discover that the primary source of your parents' misery (work) is the same life goal they want for you. Can all the learning and angst and preparation of childhood be for this? A *job*?

Why yes, my child, it is. And you'd better just start thinking about what you're going to be when you grow up. After all, it's preschool next year and you don't want to be the only child there without a vocational calling.

Interestingly, prehistoric man didn't work very hard at all. He probably *could* have put more time into stockpiling food for the hard times ahead, setting extra traps, doing odd jobs around the cave and conducting the occasional stocktake; he probably didn't *need* to take hundreds of years to fashion a sharper piece of flint.

But frankly, what would have been the point of that? He had enough to get by *and* he had the afternoons for kicking back and playing with his navel hair.

Working hard is not innate to the human psyche. It is a relatively new social construct thrust upon us by the forces of capitalism and the Industrial Revolution. Since human labour first became a unit of production, managers and economists have teased out its capacity, tested its breaking point, and kept things running as close as possible to the productive side of burnout.

Human conditioning did much of the rest, insidiously accepting over time that a full day's work was fundamental to maintaining order in daily life, while also responding to the dangling carrots of false prestige and social importance. In short, it's been a quick little jaunt in history that has taken us from owning time to time owing.

Nowadays, a job isn't just what you *do*; it's who you *are*. When Eddie Maguire introduces the next contestant on *Who Wants to be a Millionaire*, he doesn't say, 'This is Jim Collins, a shy sort of chap who likes the feel of grass between his toes, the sound of his grandchildren opening their Christmas presents, and reading old Peanuts comics'. He says 'This is Jim Collins, an accountant from Canberra'. Instantly, we all have an image of a bespectacled Jim bent over a spreadsheet and dreaming of the next time he will ravish his wife in the missionary position.

So now it's important to choose a job that will not only attract a decent wage but also define you favourably in the social spectrum. Let's face it, no girl is going to take a guy home to meet the parents if he works in a prison or prepares bodies for open caskets. You've either got to do something impressive, work for someone who's impressive, or make up something impressive.

This becomes increasingly difficult the more complex life becomes. Nowadays there are literally thousands of job descriptions one can choose from and oodles of ambiguous social tags

Mediocrity Hall of Fame
Member: Peter Finlay

Thousands of would-be and already-are writers have toiled for years to snare literature's most prestigious prize, but none with less finesse, less effort and less care than Peter Finlay (aka DBC Pierre), the Australian-born winner of the 2003 Booker prize. Soon after winning the coveted gong, Finlay was exposed as a gambler, drug addict and property shyster, none of which stopped him from turning out *Vernon God Little*, a darkly comic pearler of a yarn.

'My youth was an incredibly deviated and misenergetic affair', Finlay said in accepting his award.

To be honest, if there's a single pressure that has brought me to writing, it is regret. That's like rocket fuel for this kind of art. My theory is that when I finally purge myself of all kinds of emotions then I will probably be pretty useless as a writer. I might write an ad for Foodland.

The stunned Finlay continued:

I didn't write it to get to this point. I didn't even think it would get published. It's not a Jackie Collins and I didn't expect it to come this far. Now I just have to stay humble and talk like a wanker for a while.

that accompany them. Worse, the fickle finger of fashion has now wormed its way into the job market, thus determining *when* some jobs are cool and when they aren't.

Not so long ago the humble chippie was a grubby and uncouth sort of bloke who drank cheap beer and drove a rusty ute. Now he's a top-shelf sex symbol; the product of TV lifestyle program madness, with a nice Camry and a shiny tool belt that every man wants to copy and every woman wants to fondle. (A salient lesson indeed for all you guys who chose physics over shop B.)

When I decided to become a journalist, *60 Minutes* was unmissable television, Jane Fonda was exposing *The China Syndrome*, and newspapers didn't feature sections devoted to feng shui and cushion placement. Now *60 Minutes* employs Richard Carleton, journalists wait around for official press releases, *A Current Affair* runs weight-loss competitions, and I just don't want to talk about it anymore.

Not so long ago, IT was just a figment in the imagination of HR. Now IT is the modern answer to the previous generation's distrust of technology; a backhanded slap to quiet the disbelievers. IT is the high school chess club writ large. (Of course, one would respect IT's knowledge of 'T' if it extended beyond the insertion and retraction of a power cord, if lost files could actually be found again, and 'crashes' weren't euphemisms for 'We really don't have a bloody clue, but we certainly know a lot more about it than you do, earthling'.)

Reportedly, janitors are the next in line for corporate reinvention. Stay tuned for the IH professional—master of Institutional Hygiene, purveyor of kitchen management strategies, recycling watchdog and keeper of the spare toilet rolls.

All of which goes to show that the employment market is as prey to the whims of fashion as skirt lengths. What was hot last year is next year's wrapping paper collector at the office Christmas party. So one must ask why, given such largely uncontrollable forces and pressures, do we waste so much valuable time worrying about what we should become one day? Why do some of us devote countless years of study and sacrifice to a career that our kids won't even want us to own up to at the Preschool Parents' Day? Why, when long-haired gits who spent their twenties playing Dungeons & Dragons and rewiring old Atari machines now earn millions as compositors on *Lord of the Rings*, do we not simply head in the direction of what we enjoy and hope for the best?

Every occupation will one day have its day in the sun, its turn to shine in the fluorescent glow of corporate kudos, and this is a fact that really should be pointed out to frazzled teenagers agonising over what to do with their lives. At the end of the day, it's not what you do that ultimately counts, but what you *say* you do. 'Me? I head up the Senior Division of the Department of Carpel Tunnel Works. Oh, you want a lowly typist who'll get you a coffee? Down the hall!'

First day, first blood

Frankly, I'm amazed that anyone ever starts a job at all when you consider the horror of The First Day—those inexplicably cruel first eight hours of a new job. The federal government would do well to scratch beneath the surface of unemployment and find that all those 'lazy good-for-nothings' are actually highly motivated people rendered foetal by the prospect of The First Day at a new workplace.

The First Day collects every awkward and unpleasant emotion that one is capable of experiencing without wetting themselves, wraps them in a half-price suit, and presents the finished ensemble to a band of strange faces whose collective expression says plainly: 'We were hoping for the funny guy who was interviewed on Wednesday.'

The First Day leaves for dead the discomfort of one's first day of school because certain types of behaviour have become socially unacceptable between the two events. It's no longer cool to cry uncontrollably, to run back to the car or to bury oneself under pillows in the reading corner. There's no kind-hearted teacher around (and don't be taken in by the welcoming grin of the HR manager) to blow your nose or to sit beside you when no-one wants to have lunch with you.

And adults can be even crueller than school children. Once they've formed their little cliques within an office, you can circle around the periphery until your pen spontaneously bends—no-one gives a toss.

Why don't they care? Because they're First Day graduates! They've done the deed, felt the fear, scorched the demons and moved up in line. They're not The New Guy anymore, because YOU are. Now it's *your* sorry turn to find the toilet all by yourself.

Sure, you could always ask someone for a little early guidance and direction, but there lies a dangerous path. What if you asked The Wrong Person? For the uninitiated, The Wrong Person within a workplace is the one who will unwittingly tar you with the brush of uncoolness. This person is broadly disliked and avoided, usually with some justification. They may be a work-shirker, a buck-passer, a bum-kisser, or maybe they simply smell. Whatever the case, they're bad news and will drag you to the bottom of the heap faster than you can say internal transfer.

There is, of course, a beautifully mediocre solution to avoiding The First Day, and that is to skip it entirely by calling in sick and rolling up on the second day. No-one would accuse you of pulling a fake sickie so early in the piece; in fact, they'll probably feel compassion that you should have experienced such a shaky start to your new career. They may even take you under their wings and invite you to weekend barbecues. Many months later you can humorously reveal over a number of drinks how you deliberately avoided The First Day and went to the movies instead. The office legend is born!

The grim reaper wears a security pass

> *It's true hard work never killed anybody, but I figure why take the chance?*
> (former) **US President Ronald Reagan (1911–2004)**

Naturally I'm just being silly when I advocate avoiding work altogether. Work is a great place to pilfer stationery, engineer romance and doodle best-selling novels well before it even rates as a vital funding source. I'm just saying there's no need to get carried away with it. And I mean that quite literally. Excessive work, in which category I include unnecessary work, other people's work and work that eats into drinking time, can kill you. It really can.

The internationally rated scientific journal *Personality and Social Psychology Bulletin* recently published the results of a conclusive study that showed early achievers (those who throw themselves into work from the git-go and achieve relative degrees of success) tend to have shorter life spans than people who earn success simply by hanging around long enough. On a high-profile level, the trend is particularly evident among those US presidents and governors who were elected while young, but it can also be seen among international scientists and writers who become Nobel Laureates in record time. It's also been measured that young women who win Best Supporting Actress Oscars tend to exit stage left well before their time. Less well-known is the disturbing relationship between the year a doctor of any description receives their PhD and their ultimate life span: it seems the earlier the mortar board, the sooner the camphor chest.

Why is it so? Canadian psychology researcher Professor Stewart McCann believes work-related stress is the culprit. He says the strains, challenges and obligations associated with busting a gut before the first set of hurdles can accelerate a person's natural physical and mental decline. Early success can also, he believes, cause motivational levels to peak too early, leaving one without much incentive to bat on and keep scoring runs.

In another study, the *British Journal of Ophthalmology* published results showing that power-dressing businessmen could be increasing their risk of serious eye disease and even death by wearing their ties too tight. (It shouldn't therefore hurt your own career prospects to inform your stressed-out tie-fiddling supervisor to stop playing with it or he'll go blind.)

Even Japan, a nation well-recognised for its slavish devotion to production, is finally acknowledging that too much hard work can kill. In a landmark ruling in 2001, a Japanese coroner announced that Nobuo Miuro, a forty-seven-year-old interiors fitter who regularly worked eighteen-hour days, had finally keeled over due to *karoshi*, or 'death by overwork'. Since then, hundreds of retrospective civil lawsuits, some pertaining to deaths up to fifteen years earlier, have been filed by Japanese families accusing employers of causing karoshi. With reports of up to 10 000 karoshi-related deaths occurring each year, companies are now understandably growing nervous. Some have even introduced a firm policy of one 'no overtime' day each week, wherein employees are only required to work their allotted number of paid hours (unless of course they want to stay longer). Woo, knock yourself out, Japan.

But long hours aren't just the domain of the Japanese. In Britain, junior doctors are reported to work an average of one hundred hours each week while earning the right to wave around a stethoscope. Australia is officially the second hardest working country in the OECD (Organisation for Economic Cooperation and Development)—I know, I couldn't believe it either—with almost a third of employees working in excess of fifty hours per week and at least a quarter doing times that would be illegal in Europe. (And we can't blame boofhead bosses for this. A 2003 study by Brisbane's Griffith University showed that employees themselves are mostly to blame for working longer and longer hours, citing job insecurity as the prime motivator.)

Of course the number of hours one works doesn't necessarily relate to how *hard* one works. Ergo the public service. It merely gives an indication of how long one is prepared to sit at the same desk and cover up magazines with fake memos. Some people are better at this than others. Those who are very good at it tend to proceed to management positions very quickly. The impression is that they worked hard to get to where they are; the reality is they are more than likely highly gifted in the fields of delegation, buck-passing and Secret Santa tampering.

As one ostensibly intelligent man (who nevertheless lacked the commonsense to ask for a decent trim) once formularised: 'If A is success in life, then A equals x plus y plus z, where work is x, y is play and z is keeping your mouth shut.' It shouldn't have taken Einstein to figure that out.

It's training, it's pouring

You might think you're being treated like an idiot when management takes you on a two-day 'positivity' seminar or a week-long kumbaya-fest. You're right. You are. It's criminal.

Incredibly, the same dimwits who stand before you at weekly sales meetings and tell you that your hard-won customers will greatly appreciate the company's upcoming hike in prices and cut in basic services, will have decided that *you* need a bit of corporate coaching, a bit of workplace whipping-into-shape. And these are the people who get the decent parking spaces?

But if you thought corporate retreatism had stooped to its lowest of lows in the late-nineties, think again. There are now companies like Andrew McFarlane's LeadChange (yet another firm who thinks it's tickety-boo to push together small words and create a bigger word with a capital in the middle) which are so

Mediocrity Hall of Fame
Member: Donald Rumsfeld

Reports that say that something hasn't happened are always interesting to me. We know there are known knowns: there are things we know we know. We also know there are unknown unknowns: that is, we know there are some things we do not know. But there are also unknown unknowns: the ones we don't know we don't know.

And that's the sort of oratory that should earn you a guernsey as the next US Secretary of State—if you happen to be interested in the job, that is. Donald Rumsfeld uttered those lines to win himself the 2004 Foot In Mouth Award, an international accolade sponsored by the Plain English Campaign, a British pressure group that lobbies for straightforward language in all walks of life.

Rumsfeld should be proud, for in 2004 he faced tough competition. Actor-turned-California governor Arnold Schwarzenegger gave him a run for his money with: 'I think that gay marriage is something that should be between a man and a woman.' Indeedy.

convinced that mindless corporate training represents pay dirt, they've taken the whole concept to pasture. Literally.

LeadChange has in fact persuaded some of Britain's biggest players—among them, Deloitte, Barclays and British Telecom—to spend gazillions on . . . wait for it . . . horse-whispering courses. Yes, horses know far more about managing the bottom line than humans do, so it makes sense (neigh?) to turn to them for sage advice on forging ahead in one's chosen career.

Participants on LeadChange courses are set tasks to perform with a horse, based on a volunteered deficiency in their management style. So if you're, say, concerned about your ability to manage inter-office rivalry, skyrocketing stationery costs and shareholder revolt, you could, like, trot or something. Yes, challenges on the average horse-whispering course (cost: A$1050 per day) range from moving a horse within a pen to guiding two or three horses around an arena. You're permitted to do this via subtle touches, body language and facial expressions. You cannot simply say, 'For shit's sake, MOVE!', and more's the pity.

Apparently horses are such brilliant creatures that they will automatically detect someone who is a born leader. Unless of course it's someone other than the boss, because that'd just be silly.

Theoretically, horse-whispering is another inspired manifestation of applied industrial relations psychology and corporate insight. Realistically, it's how overpaid CEOs assuage their guilt at not having thrown a few more dollars at the ranting homeless guy outside their train station each morning. He too will one day become a corporate training guru with a kick arse hard-luck story and a quirky corporate theory.

What modern workers really need training in is the art of looking busy. Let's face it, ninety per cent of the world's work is done by ten per cent of its people; the rest of us are just showing up and flogging stationery. As economic philosopher Lord Bertrand Russell pointed out in his groundbreaking 1932 essay on work and leisure, technology has made it possible to enormously diminish the amount of labour required to secure the necessities of life. He used the following analogy to illustrate his point: imagine that at any given moment a certain number of people are engaged in making pins. They make as

many pins as the world needs, working eight hours a day. A machine is then created that enables the same number of people to make twice as many pins. In a sensible world, everyone concerned in the manufacturing of pins should now work four hours a day instead of eight. But in the real world, this doesn't happen. Instead, the workers still put in eight hours and there are too many pins produced, already at cost. Soon enough, some employers go bankrupt and half the world's pin workers are put out of work. The upshot: half the workforce is idle, unable to afford leisure; the other half is overworked, unable to find time to scratch themselves. Misery all 'round instead of happiness. As Lord Bertrand put it, 'Can anything be more insane?'

The capacity of production technology to reduce necessary work hours has only become more pronounced since Russell published his seminal essay. There are now more wage-earners per family, fewer kids to raise and more machines for mass production. Work is no longer what we need, it's what we do. And it's fair to say that a great many of us have very little to do indeed. Oh sure, we might *say* we're terribly busy, we might even feel it most days, but that's only because we've got forty-three irrelevant emails to respond to and fifteen inconsequential meetings to attend. If we stopped doing these things tomorrow, our employers would have no less trouble turning out their weekly quota of widgets.

But of course it doesn't pay not to look busy. You could get sacked and then you'd have no money, no friends, no weekend and no stationery. Having a job is important—ideally not as one of the ten per cent doing all the *real* work—so it's worthwhile learning how to look busy enough to make those wasted hours fly by. If only someone would pay me, I would happily offer the following two-year training plan to workers in need of a little guidance . . .

Ten ways to fake a good work ethic

1   Keyword: reports. Get some of these. There's bound to be some old ones in a filing cabinet somewhere. Toss several across your desk in a can't-contain-the-madness kind of way, including one right in front of you with a highlighter pen resting on top. Highlight purposefully whenever supervisors are hovering. And don't worry: curious colleagues will be so afraid they've missed a key memo, they'll never ask what's got you so flustered. Meanwhile, is too much Minesweeper ever enough?

2   Tell your mother to ring you whenever she has something new to report about the neighbours. Tell her in advance not to

worry when you answer calls with, 'Barry, you're killin' me with these margins' and, 'Hey, I never signed off on that!'

3   Try to pass out each night with your face planted in a rough-hewn cushion. It creates permanent weight-of-the-world furrows in your brow.

4   Occasionally it's a good practice to arrive at work early, but there's little point if no-one knows about it. Be sure to send a number of emails to your supervisor the minute you walk in the door and if your software permits, underline and bold the time the email was sent and mark the message, 'Urgent!' If you're stuck for something to write, try mentioning you're concerned the carpark security guy doesn't appear to start work until 6.30 a.m.

5   Turn up fifteen minutes late for after-work drinks. This shows you really must be busy while also ensuring the first shout isn't yours.

6   Ask workmates to rub your back at regular intervals. Explain that you literally don't have time to scratch yourself.

7   Develop a code system for your Post-it Notes. Write 'Remember Mum's birthday' as 'Cross-reference cost flow data 97-01', and 'Haircut Friday' as 'Don't forget! Stats review Monday! Full system back-up!! Delta force 10!!!'

8   Offer to be the one who screens all unsavoury material being emailed to company employees. Explain to your boss that workplace porn and dirty jokes spread via email are eroding the company's bottom line and that, personally, you won't stand for it.

9   Request a new ergonomically designed mouse for your computer on the basis that the old one is giving you RSI. Behold the forests of paperwork headed your way from the HR, Workplace Health & Safety and Tech Support departments. The

entire process should take you about four months, and while it won't exactly be fun, it sure ain't productive enough to be anything like hard work.

10 Move into middle management.

I'm okay, you're, *okay*, considerably more successful

It's a common misconception that very successful people are also highly intelligent; that they know something about extracting cream from corn that the rest of us don't. Certainly, one would assume it takes more than a heartbeat and a hope in hell to achieve fame and fortune, but how then to explain Pamela Anderson? Or George W. Bush? Or the entire royal family for that matter?

But what is intelligence anyway? If it's to be measured by IQ, then technically my husband is brighter than me, and frankly that's absurd. The man can't even change a toilet roll. We made the marital mistake of sitting for Australia's first national televised IQ test in 2002. Of course, the test didn't ask any of the really important questions like, 'If all your socks live in your sock drawer, then where should be the first place you look for them before you announce to the world that clearly you no longer own any?' or, 'How do you think your dirty undies make it from the bathroom floor to the washing machine each day—astral travel?', so naturally my husband excelled.

I've not heard anything else for three years. Eventually he may stop referring to himself as 'The Better Half', but I doubt I'll ever reclaim the right to choose a Saturday night video or work out which size pizza to order. 'Let's just leave all the thinking up to me then, shall we', he'll say with a knowing wink. I may have to have him shot.

Mediocrity Hall of Fame
Member: Lord Bertrand Russell

In 1932, economic sage and social commentator Lord Bertrand Russell wrote the serious version of *You take the high road ...*, Chapter 3. Through research even more, ahem, thorough than my own, Russell argued that there is far too much work done in the world, and that immense harm can actually result from the belief that work is virtuous. Specifically, he argued that the definition of full-time work should be reduced from eight to four hours a day, thereby giving people more leisure time without in any way impacting on their capacity to produce as many products and services as they quantifiably need.

Russell points out that, historically, man's concept of work was epitomised by the 'Slave State'. In pre-industrial times, whatever surplus was produced by workers beyond their subsistence needs was automatically appropriated by warriors and priests. When there was no surplus, warriors and priests still took their haul and left workers to starve. This philosophy—that leisure is the prerogative of a small privileged class and that workers have no business desiring any activity but work—lived well beyond its use-by date, the Industrial Revolution, with the result being that the modern workforce operates only a few lashes short of slavery conditions. Okay, he was a bit of a drama queen our Bertrand, but you get his drift.

Importantly, events such as World War I exemplified Russell's argument: when all men and women engaged in combat-related positions were withdrawn from productive occupations, the result was that the general level of wellbeing among unskilled allies was higher than before or since. In his words: 'The war showed conclusively that by the scientific organisation of production, it is possible to keep modern populations in fair comfort on a small part of the working capacity of the modern world. Only a foolish ascetism, usually vicarious, makes us continue to insist on work in excessive quantities now that the need no longer exists.'

Make no mistake, Lord Bertrand Russell was a lazy bastard, but at least he had justification for his malaise. And for all his affiliation with history's large working class, he credits much of mankind's progress to the much smaller 'leisure class', or really just to kicking back in general. 'The leisure class enjoyed advantages for which there was no basis in social justice ... but it contributed nearly the whole of what we call civilisation,' he said. 'It cultivated the arts and discovered the sciences; it wrote the books, invented the philosophies and refined social relations. Without the leisure class, mankind would never have emerged from barbarism. In a (future) world where no-one is compelled to work more than four hours a day, the work exacted will be enough to make leisure delightful but not enough to produce exhaustion.'

Don't get up. You're doing great things from that hammock.

I knew it would be a mistake to participate, but it's almost irresistible, isn't it? The lure of knowing how smart you really are. The possibility of discovering you've got a John Nash brain in Homer Simpson body; a genius hiding out in an ordinary life, probably just a few deep thoughts away from greatness. Or conversely, that you're as dumb as a plank and have managed to get away with it so far.

But really, what can one do with this information once we have it? Demand more money because our boss has been shown to have an IQ score lower than his golf handicap? Dump our dumber friends and seek out more cerebral types? Finally switch to the trickier crossword? Stop reciting 'Thirty days have September . . .' every time we have to write the date?

IQ scores have very little real currency, which is why public testing like this can only end in tears. Indeed, countless studies have shown that a person's IQ has no bigger than a twenty per cent role in how successful they ultimately are in life. It's therefore a pointless measurement and one that should remain, like age or bra size, a secret piece of personal information that is rude to ask about. (And what's more, I demand a recount.)

Interestingly, it's been said that technically intelligent people are actually dumb if they choose not to help their fellow man. Conscience might not be a traditional barometer of success—as Logan Pearsall Smith once pointed out, 'Most people sell their souls and live with a good conscience on the proceeds'—but it's certainly becoming increasingly relevant as the world spins inexorably towards a self-destructive anti-climax. These days the dearth of wisdom on offer, not intelligence, is what threatens to bring us undone faster than a badly wrapped kebab.

Having said that, acting on one's conscience fully and effectively can represent a lot of hard work. And God knows that ironing pile isn't going anywhere. Honestly, I look at all the nightly footage of organised peace rallies and less organised melees around the world and on my doorstep, and I think: where *do* they find the time? It's one thing to flick a greasy spatula at a smug Peter Costello on the telly while whipping up what's passing for dinner on a school night. It's quite another thing entirely to schedule a two-hour picketing of Parliament House in between the grocery shopping and the junior soccer semi-final. It's impossible not to admire the will of people whose

Mediocrity Hall of Fame
Member: George W. Bush

So he didn't technically win the election that first brought him to power. So his business acumen is dubious and his Dad's been covering his butt for years. So he's not the ripest banana in the bunch when it comes to stringing together a sentence or forming an original idea. None of those are the reason George Dubya makes our Mediocrity Hall of Fame. Nope, George makes the grade on the basis of his presidential performance alone. So far he's:

◎ Run up the largest deficit in US history.
◎ Presided over the largest sustained loss of jobs since the Great Depression (more than 3.3 million private-sector jobs have vanished since Bush took office).
◎ Set a new economic record for the most private bankruptcies filed in any twelve-month period.
◎ Witnessed the biggest drop in the history of the US stock market.
◎ Taken more annual vacation days than any other US President (including the entire month of August preceding the infamous September 11, 2001).
◎ Attracted more public protests (at one point, fifteen million people almost simultaneously around the world) than any other person in the history of mankind.
◎ Dissolved more international treaties than any other President.
◎ Been the first Prez to prompt the United Nations to remove America from its Human Rights Commission.

Yes, when future historians ponder why Bush became the most mediocre human being ever to win the highest office in the world, perhaps they should look to George's own appraisal of his presidential approach. In June 2003 he told the White House press pool: 'I'm not very analytical. You know, I don't spend a lot of time thinking about myself, about why I do things'. Yup, got that.

passion can't be contained within the confines of their own lounge room. Even when their public pleas seem hopelessly futile—as is often the case—they demand to be heard. They believe in the possibility of making a difference. They need, desperately, to vent.

Whenever I feel a similar urge, I usually end up having a good lie-down instead. I'm more of your sideline protester—an executor of mental Mexican waves for those people willing to go to the trouble of making pickets for their cause. (Where would I find a spare fence post?, I think. What sort of paint does one use? What time do I turn up? Bugger it, I'll put the kettle on instead.)

My protests are more of your sedentary, 'a pox on your house' kind. No less heartfelt, but certainly less demonstrative. I protest the indifference of banks by going *into* their branches and (somewhat outrageously) engaging the aid of a teller to assist with my deposits and withdrawals. *Yes, I know I could use the machine outside, but today I'd prefer you justify my monthly account-keeping fees, OKAY?*

I embargo all products made by Nestlé, although I can't for the life of me remember why. I refuse to buy processed chicken products because I suspect there are enough hormones flying about this house already. I write letters to the editors of community newspapers about composite classes, park facilities, aged care places and other issues that all seem terribly important at the time. Most are never printed. I've also been known to have the occasional weekly rant via my newspaper columns, although this generally backfires via a barrage of feedback letters from rattled readers. (Thank you Margaret Feltham of Wollongong. I'm sure others will follow.)

Pathetic efforts, perhaps. But efforts nonetheless. Yes, I'm still mad as hell, but I just can't fake it anymore. It's not that I don't care. I simply care from my chair. Feel free to join me over here on the couch.

Emotional intelligence

According to today's 'success coaches', the new standard measure of a person's propensity for success in life is EQ, or emotional intelligence. Many large workplaces are now being actively encouraged (by those nimrods in HR) to seek out new employees with high EQs.

So if, like most of us, you're not naturally blessed with exemplary skills in the control of your behavioural whims and tolerance for sheer stupidity and boofheadism, don't panic. Following is a handy cheat's guide, derived from the advice of EQ's creator Dr Reuben Bar-on, for espousing EQ at work without actually trying hard or having a clue:

Reuben says: Identify key people who could be useful when difficulties occur.

Mediocrity decrees: In budget meetings, sit beside the guy with the oversized calculator. During fire drills, run behind small people who would be easy to step over. Always befriend receptionists: one day they will inherit the earth.

Reuben says: Give feedback, not criticism.

Mediocrity decrees: Say 'Bob, I think your ability to conduct productive meetings while completely oblivious to the fact that everyone thinks you're a tool is an outstanding character trait'.

Reuben says: If someone is shouting, don't shout back.

Mediocrity decrees: Calmly and peacefully inform them that you know a guy called Barry who can rip out a man's voicebox with one hand.

Reuben says: Be available.
Mediocrity decrees: Say 'Of course I'm free! How's next Easter for you?'
Reuben says: Acknowledge new ideas even if they're hopeless.
Mediocrity decrees: Say 'Good to see you thinking, Jan! God knows that brain needed a run'.
Reuben says: In times of uncertainty, keep everyone informed.
Mediocrity decrees: Say to your colleagues 'I am about to go to the toilet again, but hopefully only for a number one. I try to save the number twos for home'.

That's it! I quit

So we've established that work does have an important role to play in life, provided of course it isn't too hard and that you're surrounded by enough idiots to make it occasionally fun. Work is nothing without healthy dollops of mediocrity flying about; it's that simple. But there does come a time when work has to stop. And the trouble with today's society is that it never does. Work hours and non-work hours have become so inextricably entwined that you may as well install a swinging door between your bedroom and the boardroom. The modern worker has breakfast at their desk, lunch on the run and spreadsheets with their peas at dinner.

This would be marginally less ludicrous if we still had the golden carrot of retirement to look forward to—all those mad fun hours to be had between the doctor's surgery and the gardenia patch. But even that now looks to be at risk with economic commentators speculating that an end to full-time retirement is nigh. While pure demography is partly to blame— in Australia's case, the nation is ageing faster than our capacity to knock up new bingo halls—there is also the widely touted argument that old people simply don't know what to do with themselves anymore.

Certainly, a summary look at the retirees I know does indeed reveal a few startling similarities among them: namely, weekly diaries filled with a plethora of banal and unsatisfying activities (census collecting, library shelf-stacking, picking up bratty grand-kids from school), an unhealthy fascination with the weather, and a disturbing love-hate relationship with clocks. These people seem stuck between a rock and a hard place: the immovable nugget of their available finances and the fear of doing simply nothing. But is sending them back to work the answer?

Hell no! The problem that needs fixing here is that the nation's elderly need retraining in the art of doing nothing. I mean, this is what they used to dream about; what their children now dream about. This is the chance to legitimately get off the treadmill, kick back, reflect, relax, veg out, absorb mean-ingless television and literally watch the grass grow (that's right, you don't have to fertilise it, it will grow by itself).

After two-thirds of a lifetime of hard slog, after decades of juggling family and work, of kicking goals, copping setbacks, losing one's hair through stress and lying awake at night worrying about other people's problems, *now* is the time to be selfish. Now is the time to down tools and hit that Jason recliner at full speed.

Doing nothing is a reward, not a punishment. It won't kill anyone and it won't even cost very much. Sure, it might sound boring, but that's probably because you're not doing it right.

We shouldn't be wasting the nation's resources teaching the elderly how to design kick arse PowerPoint presentations. We should be teaching them how to relax! We should be showing them how to eat, drink and be merry; to stop and smell all those roses they've planted and pruned; to whittle wood and polish off that Grandfather Port. More importantly, we should be encouraging them to feel good about their new-found idleness, not bad just because crusties like John Laws and Richie Benaud don't know when to say when. As Leonardo da Vinci so wisely put it: 'A life well spent *is* long.'

And why even wait until retirement? If you're not happy in your job, why not just quit? Quitting is not the coward's way out, despite what you've heard preached to misfit junior ice hockey teams in films starring Emilio Estevez. It is in fact an excellent back-up plan, a sound life decision, and quite often the only way you'll attract the amount of attention you've long deserved.

Take Brian Henderson, the Sydney news presenter who retired after forty years of reading an autocue. There were gala tributes, fireside interviews, lifestyle-show specials and even a guard of honour as Brian took his seat at the news desk for the last time. You would have thought the Queen was hanging up her corgi leash. Here he was—a man whose entire career had relied on him being bland and uninteresting enough to never detract from the news . . . and now he *was* the news! And no-one was going to take away his fifteen minutes of hard-earned fame, goddamnit, even if it had come at the high price of quitting the job he adored.

Yes, far from being the gesture of defeat that self-help books like to paint it as, quitting can be downright clever. Far from simply saying 'I'm finished', quitting says 'Hey! Over here, guys!', drawing back the attention that had started to pall.

Nothing, for example, more effectively reminds a jaded public about the existence of a faded sports star than the announcement he's hanging up his boots (never mind that he hasn't worn them for three years and couldn't get a run in the Gundagai Gladiators if he tried). Officially quitting, as opposed to fading quietly to black, reminds everyone that he's here, that he's ready to be added to the list of candidates for *This Is Your Life*, and that a testimonial dinner wouldn't be out of the question. Sometimes quitting is the only way to get noticed at all. Who even knew that the shy girl in Accounts Payable existed until her farewell lunch and the whip-around for her goodbye pressie?

Quitting also paves the way for that other great attention-grabbing possibility: the comeback. As the biography of Nene King attests, the magazine queen had more farewells than Barbara Streisand during her time in the Packer fold, regularly taking her bat and ball and marching home in disgust, where she would then sit by the phone and wait for the call to beg her to return. Naturally, each comeback would bring with it better pay, a longer title and a far greater appreciation for Nene's self-sacrificing dedication.

So to completely bastardise everything your mother ever taught you about winners never quitting and quitters never winning and everybody hating quitters, I'd like to proffer the possibility that inside every true winner is a serial quitter with a nose for good timing and fresh opportunity.

Try it sometime. And don't forget your bat and ball.

Chapter 4

The essentially ordinary guide to love

Love is the fart
Of every heart
It pains a man when tis kept close
And others doth offend, when tis let loose.
John Suckling (1609–42)

Dr John Gray's revolutionary discovery—that men are actually from Mars and women are from Venus—highlighted some of the fundamental travel problems involved in forging meaningful modern relationships. By understanding each other's inherent differences, Gray argued, and by working much harder to bridge the troubled space gas in between, love could find a way.

But men and women already work incredibly hard at forging and maintaining relationships, and the stats aren't getting any better. Almost half of us will get divorced at least once these days, forty per cent of us will embark on extramarital affairs (add twenty per cent if you count those people who inadvertently start Internet relationships while ordering their groceries online), and relationship counselling offices are now standing room only. Could it be that we're actually trying *too* hard, analysing every unreturned phone call within an inch of its life and workshopping the romance out of every last bunch of service station carnations? What if, instead, men and women simply accepted that love is difficult, that 'forever' is speculative at best and that no amount of complicated emotional algebra is going to make the equation any easier to apply?

Perhaps by adopting a more mediocre approach, by lowering our expectations and settling for something left of wonderful, love could become a tad more enjoyable, if no more successful.

The first kiss is the deepest

It's a little-known sociological fact that one's first snog tends to dictate the course of love until we die. Armed with this information, I would never have pashed Ashley McCarthy and his many cold sores in the banana trees at the back of his house when I was six, but there you go. You get infected, you learn.

Another thing they don't tell you is that as bad and as messy and as awkward as a First Kiss can be, it is in fact life's pinnacle of passion. Never again will you have the weight of so much anticipation, so many electrifying nerves or so much forearm-sucking practice infusing a moment with so much dramatic tension. It is, quite simply, all downhill in single-file from there.

Oh sure, kissing a new person is always a bit of a thrill. A fresh taste of lickety-spit; a glimpse of new technique. But it can never compare to that first raw, breathless, clueless kiss. And it can never undo what seeds were sown with that kiss; what future patterns of love were woven into the tapestry of tongues.

Perhaps this is why rebirthing has become such a popular brand of weirdness today. People have become desperate to rewrite history, to set new life patterns that emerge from those defining moments such as a First Kiss. If I could just have my time over again, they figure, I would wait until *after* my braces had come off, or *before* I went on the rollercoaster, or try it *without* the aid of Vaseline.

My physiotherapist friend Glenda believes, quite rightly, that her love life went pear-shaped the moment after she kissed Darrell Simpkins on the chin in the back row of the cinema in grade nine. She knew it was his chin because this is where he had been sporting a bandaid when they first walked into the darkened theatre.

Having missed his mouth and copped his chin, Glenda recoiled in embarrassment, stifled a laugh by covering her mouth and discovered the offending bandaid dangling from her lip. That Darrell then replaced said bandaid should have been Glenda's first sign that perhaps Darrell wasn't the dream date she had been saving herself for. Yet gallantly she persevered. Glenda waited for a blinding snow scene in the film (it was her only chance of seeing anything) to salvage her much-anticipated First Kiss moment. She pulled back her lips and encouraged Darrell to do the same, after which point they turned to face one another and commenced docking.

'Awwgh SHITTT!!' yelled Darrell, as the impact of Glenda's exposed teeth hitting his sent shockwaves of pain from his mouth to his groin to his toes and back again. 'What are you? Mr Ed for chrissakes?!'

Glenda was horrified, not least of all because she had distinctly felt a tooth chip during the shattering exchange, but also because Horsehead was apparently blaming *her* for this debacle. She considered debating the issue, but quickly decided things could only get worse from here and so left the theatre as fast as one can with chewing gum stuck to their jeans.

It goes without saying that Glenda has grown up with an almost pathological fear of horses. She also brushes her teeth four times a day—the objective being to gradually file them back more than to actually clean them.

More importantly, the adult Glenda is perennially unlucky in love, having developed a phobia about intimacy that sees her freeze up over romantic dinners and hyperventilate in dimly lit rooms. She is only comfortable touching men in the comfort of her consulting room and only if they have seriously buggered up their knees.

Well may she trot out this disastrous tale at late-night dinner parties to the hilarious delight of guests and friends, but anyone can see that Glenda's First Kiss is the root of all her problems (the main problem being her lack of roots). She will never get over it, or around it or past it, and really the best she can hope for in life is a mildly dysfunctional Internet relationship.

Mincing words on the 'meet' market

It has been suggested by well-meaning friends that Glenda enrol herself in one of those modern self-help-style dating courses, an example of which is the 'How To Flirt Workshop' offered by international body language consultant Harriet Juniper. Ms Juniper's admirable skill at complicating something men and women have been doing since first locking eyes across a crowded cave has won her bootfuls of cash from jaded loveless types who think there must be something they're not doing right in trying to win the attention of potential suitors.

Truth is they're probably just ugly. And that's okay because there are plenty of similarly plain folk around who are no doubt also hanging around those unflattering all-steel-and-chrome bars wondering if their casual hair flick manoeuvre is up to

scratch. It's only a matter of time before you both reach for the same Midori and pineapple juice and fall madly in love, lust, or just over.

I doubt a single customer has found the partner of their dreams as a direct result of Ms Juniper's seven-step program. For starters, there is no step that simply says 'Get drunk at Christmas party and throw oneself at colleague'. Instead, Juniper offers tips such as, 'Sit asymmetrically—it spells out *intrigue* and *individuality*' (though not necessarily *bright*) and, 'Ask for help—a light, the time, directions, anything'—a shag perhaps?

She further advises that 'When making conversation, ask questions that need more than a yes/no answer'. Because that's the great thing about nightclubs and singles' bars, isn't it? They're so conducive to intimate banter. Go on, practise this at home for Harriet Juniper's sake: cup both hands tightly, place them around the ear of the imaginary person you're talking to, muster a guttural roar from the base of your belly and scream as if your very life depends on it: 'Hey, what's your view on the application of GST to sanitary products?!'

The apparently insatiable demand for courses like Harriet's relies heavily on the public's belief that the dating well is drying up; that there's simply not enough 'product' to go around anymore. Women especially are constantly informed that there is a dearth of non-incarcerated single types left out there and that they'd better just get botoxing, networking, texting and flirting their too-big butts off before they're left on life's Big Single Shelf to rot.

But statistically this makes no sense. A large-scale study by KPMG has found that for women, at least, a veritable glut of single men (at least 727 000 aged twenty-five to thirty-four) is just waiting to get the call-up. They may not all be Jamie Durie, but they're not all Chopper Read either. The fact is there are more than enough available men and women out there, but no-one is ever going to find anyone if we continue to allow so-called love experts, self-help gurus, contrived compatibility systems and commercial dating services to complicate what is essentially a very basic activity.

The simple act of meeting someone has gone all Excel spreadsheety on us, producing hybrid versions of itself that unite technology and business-speak in ways that are downright frightening. Between SMS-based services that promise to find your perfect match via random text messaging (I luv U, who R U?) through to online chatrooms and cyber square dances, the basic goal of meeting someone now requires a post-grad IT degree and a computer that will fly you to the moon.

Even speed dating, widely promoted as the stress-free alternative to longwinded and expensive first dates, is based on the concept of cattle-call job interviews. Frankly, what could be more stressful?! Job interviews are just behind public speaking and root canal work on the list of things that most terrify us, so how could throwing force-fed romance into the mix make things any less stroke-inducing? How is it that finding someone has been made harder than tax law while divorce is simpler than sneezing?

Meeting people is *not* hard. They're everywhere for heaven's sake! They're in your supermarket line when you don't want them, they're clogging traffic intersections, they're blocking your view at the movies, they're buying the last pair of shorts in your size, they're impeding your view at the beach. Just because people are in your face doesn't mean they're any less single or available. One doesn't *have* to find Mr or Miss Right via contrived and complicated means. It really can be as easy as tapping on someone's shoulder and saying 'Well? How 'bout it?'

Whatever happened to the good old days when one simply got smashed at the pub, snogged a drinking buddy and moved in together when one of you got evicted? It might not be *Romeo & Juliet*, but it's got no greater chance of ending in Splitsville than exchanging email photos with <bigboybrad@hotmail.com> who lives on an iceberg off Alaska.

And one final word of advice for the girls: don't believe your Mum when she says you'll never meet Prince Charming while getting smashed in a dodgy pub. Mary Donaldson, a blow-in from Hobart, met the Prince of Denmark while losing her legs in Sydney's seedy Slip Inn. Three years later, she's got more tiaras than Don Burke has cuttings.

Hard day at the office

The great white hope for Australia's future procreation figures remains the workforce. If not for the convenience and accessibility of office romance, love wouldn't be stuffed finding a way. But even this now looks to be at risk, thanks largely to the omnipresent influence of American culture.

If Australia follows the lead of the US (a kooky stretch but work with me here), office romance could soon become a highly legislated affair. About ten per cent of American bosses have officially banned office love, while many more have instituted policies to 'regulate' it.

In fact the US corporate world is completely spooked about the flow-on effects of cubicle canoodling, with eighty-one per cent of human resource managers declaring office romances 'dangerous' and thirty-nine per cent believing that public displays of affection at work should be prohibited. Bill Clinton and his mid-morning cigars clearly have a lot to answer for.

To date, Australia has adopted a much more casual approach to deskbound dalliances—and just as well. How much further would our (allegedly) appalling sickie rate escalate if we removed the promise of a good old-fashioned storeroom snog? What reason do some of us have to even show up at the office other than to either partake in or witness the act of colleagues making idiots of themselves around the photocopier?

Certainly America's implementation of 'love contracts', 'romance clauses' and 'consensual relationship agreements' has possibly lessened their chances of being hit with sexual harassment lawsuits. But at what cost a little workplace fun? And to what extent could productivity be curtailed by the dogleashing of office morale?

Moreover, how can any of us be expected to meet someone these days if we're not allowed to eye off the new person in Accounts Payable? When so many of us have to work fifteen-hour days just to pay the drycleaner, where else are we supposed to meet prospective partners? At the mailbox?

Significantly, a 2002 report by an independent marketing company revealed that almost half of all attached couples surveyed met each other through work. Convenience and accessibility are important foundations for a lasting union. That and having a lift to the office each day.

Indeed, for some people, the only incentive to get off the couch and find a job at all is the prospect of finding a work partner who might in fact have a much comfier couch at their place. The only challenge here is to target a workplace that has a good cross-section of employees, the critical mass being about twenty. (You can always pick couples forced together by the slim pickings of a small family business. You can usually pick their kids too.)

Going down the American road of legislating office romance would only force the whole scene underground anyway. And then no-one would have anything to point at, laugh at or gossip about. Internal office email networks would become redundant; so too the work Christmas party. The only thing left at work would be, well, work. And I don't have to tell you how ridiculous that would be.

In fact, my advice to corporate Australia is to actually add value to office romance by imposing a few more rules of the game. Not the killjoy regulatory-type rules that Americans favour, but rather some fun and friendly etiquette requirements such as the following:

◎ People who are obviously keen on each other must be physically separated by at least twenty metres of open office space. This ensures that fellow employees are regularly treated to the hilariously lame excuses each party finds to walk past the other's desk.

- ◎ In a world of ever-dwindling stationery supplies, workplace couples must be made to share the same stapler.
- ◎ Work couples should not be allowed to pair up in Secret Santa-style morale-boosting exercises. No-one wants to see them exchanging heart-shaped pillows and other such non-piss-taking gifts.
- ◎ When a supposedly secret couple is finally caught out publicly, they must be made to wear 'Okay! We're shagging!' T-shirts for the remainder of that week.
- ◎ When a work romance involves extramarital activity, fellow employees should be allowed to take a straw poll on who gets to tell the wronged spouse.
- ◎ When an office romance ends, employees should be encouraged to take sides, forge alliances and also change alliances without notice. If a *Survivor* series sprouts up around it, all the better.

Of course, working against the chugging office romance machine is the increasing trend towards home-based self-employment and telecommuting. For all the wonderful slacking-off benefits these initiatives provide, they are nevertheless producing a generation of lonely, isolated desperados. I know, I'm one of them. The closest thing I get to office romance these days is when my husband phones to remind me it's bin night. *Woo, settle down aorta.*

Somehow modern society needs to extricate itself from the messy love predicament in which it's landed. Between complicating the process with contrived technology, over-analysis and unnecessary how-to guides and simply rendering ourselves unavailable, the future is not looking good. The latest figures show that in every state and territory in Australia, there are now more people either single and/or living alone than ever before. It seems we're all trying harder than ever to achieve something that should be infinitely easy and actually having less success as a result. If this doesn't make a compelling enough argument to embrace a more mediocre approach to the process of finding a partner, then remember this: sitting at home on a Saturday night may not be the end of the world, but it's hardly getting you any closer to a decent foot rub, is it?

Are we having fun yet?

Once you've actually located a potential suitor, and unless you're lucky enough to find one averse to the spending of copious amounts of money on tiny meals on large white plates, there is a period of horrid and largely inescapable awkwardness that must follow. Courting is enjoying a new-millennium renaissance, having limped through the pash-and-dash eighties and cyber-sex nineties without so much as a goodnight peck. In spite of technology's

The more expensive the meal, the less of it you'll actually taste.

overwhelming pervasiveness in the area of meeting people, many new couples continue to entertain the simplicity of a traditional dinner-and-movie rendezvous as both a vehicle for getting to know someone better and for avoiding re-runs of *The Bill*.

Personally I've always found dates to be a lot like job interviews, though marginally less fun. Fraught with confusion and assumptions and second-guessing and pretence and sheer unadulterated terror, dates have the added complication of involving food.

It really doesn't matter where you grew up or how fussy your parents were; dates transport each of us back to that moment when a knife and fork or pair of chopsticks were first placed in our pudgy little hands just prior to someone losing an eye. We are rendered stupid, clumsy and utterly retarded by nerves. Suddenly that rack of lamb in beetroot *jus* (freshly *squissed* no doubt) seems like a really bad idea. There's no way you'll be getting any meat off those bones unless you're allowed to stick your foot on it and growl.

Ironically, the more expensive the meal, the less of it you'll actually taste. The pressure is simply too great to allow for the normal functioning of tastebuds. Doggy bags are clearly not an option on such occasions, but at least you'll have that great gob of steak and parsley wedged in your front teeth to sample later on.

Keeping up the conversation while eating is equally tricky. The only time you'll have something truly witty and interesting to say will be when your mouth is full of potato. Not wanting to miss your moment, you'll persevere anyway, covering the gaping mass of moving food in your mouth with your pinky finger, fooling no-one. By the time coffee rolls around, you won't have a single witty anecdote left to proffer.

The arrival of the bill takes the awkwardness quotient to an all-night high. Should the male pay, while still acknowledging the rights of women to equal pay, equal status and equal credit card debt? Should the woman pay because, well, she can? Should they go Dutch, thereby acknowledging each other's earning power, respecting each other's financial responsibilities and demonstrating their ability to divide by two? In which case, should they discuss the fact that she had a $12 risotto and he had a $26 steak but that she also swiped his bread roll when he went to the toilet and ate more than her half of their shared dessert? And might this be the best conversation they've had all night?

And do they then 'do coffee' or perhaps enjoy a drink on the way home? Will he finally get his chance to break wind? Will she be expecting a goodnight kiss and, if so, would a nipple-tweak be out of the question?

So many dilemmas . . . so little time left until *Sports Tonight* starts.

Beginner's guide to Mediocre Dating 101

1 *Things you should never order at a restaurant*

Spaghetti: There are two options here: one is to twiddle your spaghetti around a fork in a spoon until the second coming of Christ, while the other is to cut it up a-la-kindergarten style. Neither method is going to result in sex.

Chicken wings: You've never done this well at home, so why would you attempt it in company?

Pizza: Murphy's Law of Dating clearly states that you will almost certainly get both the stretchiest slab of cheese Kraft has ever produced and salami-related food poisoning.

Soup: To spoon away from or towards the body? To sip or to slurp? To leave the dregs or mop up with bread? Soup raises too many questions.

Tacos: Only advisable if you really, really don't like the other person.

Seafood: Shells, bones, weird-looking grey bits. Could anyone be worth all that effort?

2 *What to wear*

Flirting 'expert' Harriet Juniper advises keen couplets to wear clothing that is 'neat' and 'says something about you'. This is cleverly ambiguous enough to ensure you can't possibly sue her when next you're left standing cold and alone at the front of a restaurant in your socks and sandals. The simple mediocre fact is that wearing a smart dress-shirt and suit with a fetching tie will signal to your date that you're going places. Wearing a fetching tie without the shirt and suit says you're going to a wedding tomorrow, probably your own. Wearing your brother's puffy pirate shirt, your mother's latest attempt at stretch-sewn trousers and your favourite Dunlop sneakers complete with Liquid Paper touch-ups says you're going to spend your fortieth birthday at a backyard barbecue with two of your closest friends and your father's Rotary pals. Girls, wear a push-up bra and a dress that says 'I couldn't possibly fit a purse anywhere on my person. Please pay'.

3 *What you should talk about*

There are basically two groups of people at restaurants: newly courting couples anxious to fill the gaps in conversation and bored married types for whom conversation is just one long gap. The former group will all too soon be the latter group, so it would pay for them to quit the desperate grappling for cerebral date chat and instead take a shortcut or two to successful gap-filling. May I suggest the following timeless openers?

- What *is* the difference between a Labrador and a Golden Retriever?
- Does the light stay on when the fridge door shuts?
- How come all the Popes look the same?
- Given that we can land on the moon, why do aeroplanes still need such a long run-up?
- Cats. Why?
- What if he's heavy *and* he's my brother?
  Hmmm. Frisky?

4 *Who should pay?*

In a perfectly mediocre world, this wouldn't even be a question. The one with the most ludicrously ill-advised credit card limit would pay. But in the real world, crazy norms and unspoken etiquette come into play, leaving the average punter hopelessly uninformed and dangerously wallet-exposed.

The mediocre question should not be, 'Who should pay?' but rather, 'Should we pay?' In other words, there are many, many dead-easy ways to escape payment for a meal and these should be eagerly exploited by the new couple-in-waiting. Undercooked meat, lumpy potatoes, too-small mains, too-large entrees, a Greek salad that looks frightfully Italian . . . all funny and frugal anecdotes to share for years to come. Sure, you're unlikely to make any other couple friends with this sort of form, but like you want to do that whole bill-splitting thing anyway.

> **5 *How to bail early***
>
> The traditional way of cutting short a nightmare date is to surreptitiously signal a waiter to summon you to an urgent phone call from a close relative who needs urgent attention and just happened to know you were dining at Toong Tong Thai tonight. Sometimes the classics are the best. Stick with this one.

Gettin' jiggy with it

So why do we endure the mental anguish and emotional second-guessing that defines the courting process? The answer is, of course, rumpy-pumpy. Yes, as evolved as we like to think we are, humans remain servant to the basic primal instinct of physical gratification, a consideration well before the exchange of benefactor signatures on a superannuation form.

In much the same way that we have complicated other basic primal instincts, such as eating and erecting shelter, man has turned sex into an increasingly fraught affair. It is the great undoer of both drawstring pants and otherwise healthy relationships.

Quite possibly, the tampering started back in India around the third century when a handful of toey types with time on their hands established the foundations of Tantric sex. They surmised that lovemaking had become too outcomes-focused; too much about the destination and too little about the journey. Accordingly, they sought to develop some time-intensive techniques that made the final goal less important, or even did away with it altogether.

While admirable in its intent, this approach dangerously challenged men's innate cannonball approach to sexual gratification (Ready? I am! Fire!), while also planting the seed in women's minds that perhaps they weren't getting all they were entitled to on the coital front. Right or wrong, things have been hopelessly messy ever since.

Case in point: in the 2003 Australian Study of Health and Relationships, published by a conglomerate of national universities and research centres, almost fifty per cent of men surveyed and seventy-two per cent of women confided that they had experienced some sort of prolonged 'sexual difficulty' in the past year. These ranged from flagging libido to body image concerns, phobias, physical pain and that old camping clanger—the stubborn tent peg. Yet at the same time, we're right up there in the horny nation stakes, following only Hungary and France in Durex's annual international bonkometer survey. It seems forty-seven per cent of us might be faking our orgasms Down Under, but at least we're faking them three times a week. We'll take our sex like our cricket, thanks, unorthodox but prolific.

Sex is a relatively simple assembly procedure that should not be confused with moon jaunts or astral travel.

But who can trust sex surveys anyway? No-one ever tells the truth in them, and those who do are most likely statistical anomalies. For a start, people who have time to fill out a sex survey either (a) don't have children and therefore don't require the perfect biennial alignment of opportunity, motive and desire, or (b) are angst-ridden *Dolly*-reading fourteen-year-olds who think they're missing out on something.

When I read in a national newspaper that the average Australian couple is managing a doona dance at least three times a week, I laughed all over my cereal. Their pants are either on fire or things have gotten so desperate they're now counting fly-by-the-cheek morning kisses as would-be riotous romps.

Certainly, a quick anecdotal survey of my friends and neighbours yielded a far different response. Most are so flat out *finding* a pair of trousers most days that they're hardly likely to risk removing them, while others have given up on ever reclaiming the vast portion of their bed now permanently colonised by a succession of toddlers, Tickle-Me-Elmos and limbless Action Men.

Some couples are emotionally scarred by this unexpected reality, but others have mercifully accepted what is ordinary, mediocre and inexplicably true. Sex is a relatively simple assembly procedure that should not be confused with moon jaunts or astral travel. Just as Henry Miller once accused D.H. Lawrence of 'building the Taj Mahal around something as simple as a good f***', men and women today could be accused of ascribing too much symbolism and too many expectations upon something only marginally more satisfying than a completed game of Scrabble.

At the end of the day, sex is *not* like it is in the movies—wild, wanton and sans kitten breath. As author David Lodge once said, 'Literature is mostly about having sex and not much about having children. Life is the other way around'.

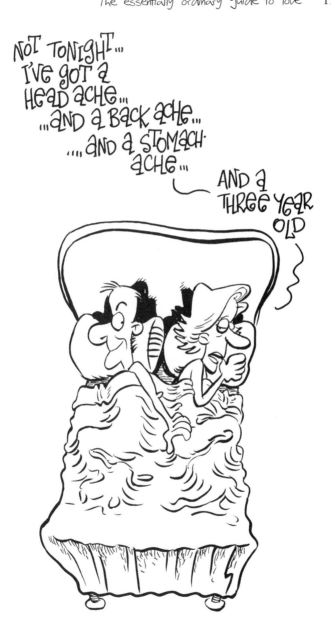

The mediocre guide to getting out of sex

Man may have landed on the moon, pioneered the Internet and squeezed whipped cream into a can, but as far as sexual excuses go we're still living in the Dark Ages. 'Not tonight, dear, I have a headache' is still the most favoured rationale of the unwilling, closely followed by 'I'm too tired', 'But it's that time of the month' and 'You can't *honestly* be serious'. I'm sure you'll agree this is simply not good enough, and that if the crumbling institutions of marriage and monogamy stand any hope of surviving this century, we're going to have to start coming up with some much better and more solidly mediocre excuses than those lame offerings.

And so, out of respect for neglected partners everywhere, I offer you this handy new-millennium guide to Getting Out Of Sex Thoughtfully and, Okay, Pretty Shabbily . . .

For the sports lover: 'Honey, I think I've hit a form slump. Out of respect for the team, I'm going into camp. It's only for the love of the sport—and you—that I do this.'

For the new-age exerciser: 'Sorry, but I tore my chakra and twisted my inner focus during a particularly deep Floating Tree Pose today. You'll have to centre yourself tonight.'

For the sales executive: 'Look, the bottom line is that my margins have shrunk and my paradigms are all out of whack. I promise I'll have a more favourable proposal to you ASAP.'

For the pragmatist: 'It's like this. We can either do it now and miss *The Panel*, or we can actually have something other than the kids to talk about for the next week.'

For the number-cruncher: 'Did you know that twenty-four per cent of heart attacks occur on the job? I just don't want you to become another statistic, sweetheart.'

For the busy woman: 'Hey, I've heard that workshopping a relationship's emotional flaws while making love actually heightens the experience for both parties. Wanna try it?'

For the superstitious: 'I'm sorry, but I have just had this really bizarre feeling that if we have sex tonight, my mother will want to stay here for Christmas.'

Yes, good excuses are as important to a decent sex life as a watertight alibi, and it pays to remember that you're only as good as your last.

Ex marks the spot

When searching for Mr, Miss or Ms Right, it pays to ignore the advice of well-meaning magazine agony aunts and books with planets in their titles that wish to help you find that someone special who will happily change your colostomy bag in years to come. The truth is that 87.5 per cent of new relationships will either trip at the first hurdle or pull a hammy mid-race, leaving you with yet more 'mistakes to learn from', 'memories to cherish' and 'lessons for the journey', but more importantly with another real-life ex to contend with.

Unlike raging hangovers, ex-partners don't simply disappear after a strong coffee, a hot shower and a long, hard think about oneself. They keep on living, breathing and occupying space, often still on the periphery of your own now desperate-and-dateless existence. They pop up where and when you least expect them, stay in contact with your friends, hang on to words you've written as though they might be called into evidence, and generally cling to the edges of your fragile sub-conscience like bubblegum to a shoe.

Just when you think you're finally over your ex—or that he/she is over you—embarking on a new relationship will quickly draw them back into the fold. New partners, especially, okay, women, want to—no, *need* to—know about your ex. Guys, they need to know what she looked like, what sort of things you did together, what presents you exchanged, holidays you went on, plans you made, cards you wrote, how you broke up, what you've learnt from that, whether she's still in touch with you, what your parents thought of her, and most importantly, what the sex was like. None of your answers will prove satisfactory.

It is an especially good practice, regardless of whether you're the dumper or the dumpee, to remove all tangible evidence of a newly ended relationship before it has time to become absorbed into the fabric of your life, thus becoming a ticking time-bomb awaiting discovery by a new partner.

I once knew a girl who thought it incredibly sweet that her new partner kept a ratty old teddy bear on his pillow, clearly a remnant of his childhood or an endearing present from his far-away mum. When she first asked him where he acquired the teddy, he remarked, a little hesitantly, that he'd quite forgotten— it had just become a habit of his to put the 'silly thing' on his pillow each day. In the end, it took about a week of intensive

Exes don't have to boil rabbits to be an annoyance. They just have to exist.

questioning, pleading tears, stony silences, unreturned calls, hurled pillows and slamming doors to uncover the truth—that of course the teddy was a gift from his ex. He'd 'forgotten' to get to rid of it in the same way he'd 'forgotten' about his ex entirely, but would his new partner like to dismember the teddy anyway? Why, yes, thank you, she would. And I did.

That's the thing about exes. They don't have to boil rabbits to be an annoyance. They just have to exist. Their presence, even if fleeting, can cast a long shadow.

That said, some cast longer shadows than others, and some, damn it, cast really skinny shadows with perky breasts and tight butts. Which is why, getting back to my original point, it is wise to choose new partners on the basis of what kind of ex they'll make, because on the basis of odds alone, this one may not go the distance either.

Look for someone who lives a long way away, preferably in another state, or who has tentative plans to go overseas at some point in the future (chances are breaking up will give them the impetus to finally take that journey, thus blessing you with the tyranny of distance). Look for someone on the average side

Mediocrity Hall of Fame

Member: Eric Moussambani

The world loves a winner, but it loves quality losers even more. Especially if they lose in the style of Eric 'The Eel' Moussambani, who had never swum a hundred metres in one go before he did it in the heats of the Sydney 2000 Olympics' Men's one-hundred-metre freestyle competition.

The twenty-two-year-old from Equatorial Guinea didn't fancy himself completing the distance, having only taught himself to swim nine months earlier in his homeland's crocodile-infested river, but the fortuitous false starts of his two other heat contestants (from Nigeria and Tajikistan) meant that Moussambani had the Olympic pool all to himself.

Onlookers cheered wildly as Eric flailed his way down the pool, his head never once going underwater (hey, never smile at a crocodile!), and performed the most unorthodox tumble-turn in the history of competitive swimming. But jubilation turned to fear when it seemed Eric was either going to run out of puff or drown dramatically on his way back down the pool. A rescue team was about to jump in about ten metres from the finish of the race, but Eric waved them off and completed the last stretch in excruciating fashion.

Moussambani received a standing ovation from the Sydney spectators and said, when he could breathe again, that it was only the roar of the crowd that had made him finish his greatest endurance test. 'The gold medal is not everything', he told reporters. 'To me what happened today was worth more than gold.'

Sadly, however, Eric's success was fleeting, at least back in his own country. Greeted only by his parents at the airport, Moussambani was shocked to discover he had officially 'shamed' his nation by recording the slowest ever time in a one-hundred-metre race. He was banned from training in Equatorial Guinea's only swimming pool and is now forced to train in the open sea by himself.

Which he does. No tumble-turns required.

of good-looking (presentable, not unforgettable), and who is just starting to pack on the pounds. That way, if you and your new partner run into him/her in the supermarket, neither of you will dwell for too long on what you're missing or what you're competing with. Also, if it's likely you'll be the one dumped when things finally play out, he/she might not be as quick to find a new suitor now that he/she is looking scary in a g-string, thus sparing you the hideous 'I'd like you to meet my new partner, X' awkward moment.

Ideally, look for someone who is not borderline psychotic, a manic depressive, heavy drinker, junkie or potential stalker, unless of course you're likely to look back on these traits with fondness. Look for someone who has a healthy posse of family and friends, thus enabling them to step over the spot you've just vacated without really noticing. Look for someone fairly well-off—they seldom ask for their stuff back. And don't stop short of doing a quick reference check just to be sure your future ex's exes don't rate them a nightmare ex.

If all goes well and everything checks out, it's quite possible you've found yourself a moderately suitable partner—both for the future and the past. Which is as about as clever as love gets, really.

Keeping passion alive against its will

If the sex is worth going back for, marriage (or at least a long-term defacto relationship) may inevitably follow. Don't worry about becoming a statistic; it's better than living with your Mum.

You will find many helpful books around about how to make a long-term relationship work. Most are robust enough to become highly effective missiles during heated arguments over the phone bill. What these tomes won't tell you, however, is about the biggest hidden challenge lurking within any sustained monogamous relationship. I'm talking of course about the off-season. Or, as I like to think of it, the gap between the footy and the cricket—a long, dark period of awkward silences, forlorn looks out the window, and an unhealthy interest in televised golf.

The off-season sneaks up on unsuspecting couples. There you are happily witnessing your weekends fly by in a blur of can't-miss games and footy tipping chart hilarity. Your friends are always over, the TV is loud, the beer is flowing, the kids are . . . well, they were here a minute ago . . . when suddenly, almost rudely, the commentators declare footy to be the winner (again) and promise to be back next year.

Somewhere in the distance, a dog barks.

Men, it has to be said, are likely to take this blow much harder than women. But there is much a loving partner can do to help her man get through the sporting slump and therein keep her mediocre match-up alive and kicking.

First, she can help him kill the intervening time by finding him a hobby he hasn't tried before like, say, clearing the bathroom floor of fetid socks, phoning his mother without prompting, and doing an occasional headcount on the number of children presently sharing his address.

He could also, with the right amount of encouragement, use this time to expand his cultural horizons beyond *The Footy Show*. Obviously this needn't encompass anything as outlandish as a night at the theatre (it can really disturb a man when actors break into song), but certainly a trip down to the local RSL to catch the touring Roy Orbison impersonator couldn't be too traumatic.

Mediocrity Hall of Fame

Member: Ruslan Ponomariov

It's not easy to cause international uproar during a chess game, but Swedish grandmaster Ruslan Ponomariov did in 2003 when he became the first world chess champion to be officially disqualified for accidentally leaving his mobile phone turned on during a game. Should've given it one final check, mate.

Another option to direct attention away from those thumping 'Summer is coming!' cricket ads on the telly is to engage in a little sport yourselves. Why not try that wacky old game called Spontaneous Affection, or how about a walk outdoors (it's okay, the remote can come too).

Women may also need a little help throughout this difficult time. For a start, what are we actually going to talk about now that we've finally got our audience back? What was it that was so important we spent all winter moaning about the lack of opportunity to discuss it? Wasn't it something to do with the state of our relationship? The death of romance perhaps? Maybe it was just about the guttering.

At any rate, this time of year should represent a unique opportunity for men and women to take stock of their relationships; to look at one another with fresh eyes; to cast aside the TV guide, eat dinner at the table again, and discuss something other than pending tribunal decisions.

Don't worry; it's only for a few months.

Apart from such sage advice, there are really no instructions that accompany the institution of marriage, and it shouldn't therefore surprise anyone that about forty per cent of them fall apart. Yet couples still flock to the altar in their thousands. Weekends are now booked solid with 'starter' weddings (hastily aborted couplings that pave the way for a second wedding, this time with feeling), round-two atonements, third-go hopefuls and 'What the hell? I have no pride anymore' fourth-timers. Flustered florists barely have time to catch their baby's breath. Anyone would think it was illegal to throw large, fully catered parties without first getting the nod from a man of the cloth.

Whether it's men not doing enough to get it right, or women doing way too much, marriage remains the trickiest of life's conundrums. We expect big things to grow from the seed of love, but never anticipate the sheer tedium of gardening. 'From

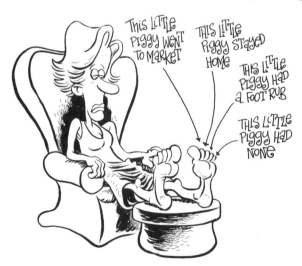

courtship to marriage', as William Congreve wrote in 1693, 'is as a very witty prologue to a very dull play'.

But perhaps the real flaw in the institution of marriage is our interpretation of what it represents: the start of a thrilling journey, the blooming phase of love. Perhaps if we instead viewed it as the *end* of a journey, as the *pruning* phase of love, we would be much happier in its comfortable embrace.

For marriage, unburdened with the expectations of falling in love again and again, really does have a lot to offer the ordinary couple, including:

◎ All the financial benefits of share-house accommodation without the restrictions on nose-picking in company.
◎ The availability of someone with whom you can comfortably order spaghetti bolognaise, chicken wings or barbecued ribs at an all-you-can-eat buffet.
◎ Double the range of socks.
◎ Someone else's dysfunctional family to compare with your own.
◎ Wedding presents, especially exchangeable ones.
◎ A second gene pool to blame for odd-looking children.
◎ A permanent excuse for having no plans on a Friday night . . . ever.
◎ Two office Christmas parties at which to disgrace oneself.
◎ Having someone who will tell you honestly when you look as bad as you feel.
◎ Having someone who will see you through numerous ill-informed hairstyles and fat phases (and in fact probably won't even notice).
◎ Having someone who will save you from the spectre of a fatal mid-air collision by vetoing all major travel plans until the home loan is paid off.

Mediocrity Hall of Fame
Member: Michael Edwards

Michael 'Eddie The Eagle' Edwards soared to new lows when he took on the best of the world in the ski jumping event at the 1988 Winter Olympics. Britain's first and only Olympic ski jumper, Eddie figured he'd have a go if no-one else would, and in doing so demonstrated to the entire world what it takes to be a champion: an obscure sport with no countryman rivals.

But this was no college-prank attempt at greatness. Despite what his many critics asserted, Eddie had never set out to make a mockery of the sport of ski jumping. He had taught himself to ski in a country with barely any skiable snow and with no-one trained to teach him. He borrowed skis, funded his own training regime and spent two years clearing double-decker buses and cheating death.

Importantly, the false success Edwards enjoyed during and immediately after the Winter Olympics (he proved a media dream with his Coke-bottle glasses, overweight physique and self-deprecating wit) translated into genuine success borne entirely of The Eagle's ski-jumping mediocrity. Edwards became a much in-demand public speaker and, while he did ultimately squander much of the financial proceeds he gained from all that media attention, he eventually knuckled down to pursue his other, less death-defying life goal of becoming a lawyer. A big-budget movie of his 1988 antics is currently in the making.

No-one will ever be able to do another Eddie The Eagle, at least not at the Winter Olympics. Sport officials have now imposed a ruling—known as the 'Eddie Rule'—that prohibits entrants who don't achieve certain heights and distances during qualifying.

So unfortunately you can't just show up anymore—but at least, in 1988, one crazy guy did.

◎ At least a snowball's chance in hell of obtaining a home loan.

◎ A reason to laugh at Homer and Marge.

◎ Someone with whom you can mock and taunt slow-moving caravans right up until the day you buy an Evinrude together.

◎ The highly effective stick of financial ruin as disincentive for indulging the whims of the office assistant.

◎ Anniversary sex.

And if it all goes to hell in a handbasket, it's not the end of the world. There's no limit on how many times you can give marriage a red-hot go, or how many times your brother will be only too happy to sleep with one of the bridesmaids, or how many celebrants to whom you can toss a guernsey.

Marriage doesn't come with guarantees or insurances or even get-out clauses. It doesn't come wrapped in a neat bow (hence 'tying the knot') and is quite possibly the most poorly worded contract in the history of binding agreements. But as long as there's free grog at weddings, people will continue to get married. And more power to them! It can't be too much fun cutting up your own meat when you're eighty-five.

Chapter 5

The essentially ordinary guide to parenting

The hand that rocks the cradle
Is the first to display arthritic tendencies.
William Ross Wallace (sort of), 1819–81

Position vacant

Cell-splitting Engineer and Development Consultant*
Salary: Neg. (as in negligible)
Bonuses: Squillions of leftover chicken nuggets, an inexhaustible number of excuses not to attend social events with people you don't actually like very much.
Qualifications: Ideally will have read *Where did I come from?*, though not essential.
The position: You will have direct responsibility for the creation and ongoing care of one or more small human beings not equipped with radar-tracking devices. These little people, known within the industry as children, will rely upon you for their every basic need and want, none of which they will be able to clearly communicate to you until much further down the track, at about which time they may in fact decide *not* to communicate with you because you are, after all, not *them* and therefore relatively unimportant in the grand scheme of things.

You will grow to love these little people more than you ever thought possible, not least of all because exchanges and/or refunds aren't accepted. This will make it infinitely easier to cope with the amount of overtime the position requires, which may include all-night vigils by a sick child's bed, midnight sheet-washing marathons, long aimless drives around dimly lit neighbourhoods at two in the morning, and later, weekends spent fashioning Mount Vesuvius out of 400 newspapers and a bucket of slop.

Much heavy lifting will be necessary. (Persons with extra limbs are especially encouraged to apply.) You will also be required to apply numerous engineering concepts, including several that defy conventional logic, such as how to load one hundred and fifty kilograms worth of nappy bags and toys onto the back of a four-gram stroller without upending the child or severing a major artery.

A medical degree will be favourably looked upon.

You will be required to sing, dance and shake colourful objects on command, and while no prior talent is necessary, fellow shoppers tend to appreciate it more if you have some.

You love twilight walks on the beach, drive-in movies, and long seafood lunches. One day you might even do these again.

It is expected that you will instinctively understand your children's psychological urges and emotional motivations, even while your own sanity is sipping pina coladas on an island off Nutsville. You will have the short-term memory of a gnat, yet with the uncanny ability to recite *Green eggs and ham* well into your eighties.

The right applicant will be able to look at a pile of milk cartons, bottle tops and tissue boxes and think, 'Tyrannosaurus Rex scale-model'. They will be similarly imaginative in the kitchen, producing seemingly endless varieties of vegetable mash from ingredients that are only sometimes related to vegetables.

You will be able to laugh in the face of your children's ungraciousness. When they suddenly won't be caught dead with you in public, you will commence walking like a chicken and yelling Tourettes-like at them to stop picking their nose and eating it. You will tell their friends about the time they pooed their pants in the long-jump pit on sports day and wrote earnest letters to TV evangelist Jimmy Swaggart. You will cop on the chin their cries that you are 'uncool' and 'old-fashioned' and 'square', and you will remind them of these taunts when they want to move back in after their first live-in relationship goes pear shaped.

You will teach them about the things that matter, though not of course about sex, which you will assume they will work out for themselves with the same degree of ritual humiliation that you did. You will teach them values and ethics, always with the outclause: 'Do as I say, not as I do'.

You will stick with this parenting thing, often running on nothing bar the smell of an old bunny rug and the faint fumes of unconditional love, well beyond the hope of a tangible reward or a simple 'Thank you'. You will understand that one of your most important roles is to serve as a source of blame and derision for your children in later years.

You must be intuitive, inspired, generous, forgiving, multi-skilled and ripe for abuse. In other words, you are quite simply amazing and no doubt far too busy to reply to this advertisement. Never mind, we're sure you would have made an outstanding employee.

* aka Parent

Maternal instinct and other barefaced lies

If one had the time, one would hunt down and beat with a nappy bag the peach-faced midwife who first assured one that parenting was going to 'kick in' shortly after birth. 'Don't worry,' the midwife sweetly told one—alright, *me*—when not for the first time I'd asked if night feeding was a task I could contract out. 'You think you know nothing now, but you'll be amazed how much knowledge just falls into place the moment you first hold that new baby in your arms. It's instinctive!'

Now I don't really subscribe to instinctive. Who can really buy the notion that humans are born with anything more intuitive than the urge to pass wind and ultimately self-destruct? I don't, for example, think for one minute that humankind would instinctively seek out new food sources if the world's resources suddenly dried up. I've seen enough couch-bound men reach the point of starvation because the nearest person with ovaries hadn't been grocery shopping for two weeks.

Having said all that, I decided to believe the midwife in question. She was, after all, a midwife; a job title I assumed was somewhere close to God. She seemed so confident that even

someone like me, someone who thought Bonjella was a kind of French dessert, would suddenly know what to do after the cord was cut. Never mind that I hadn't kept a pot plant alive in twenty-five years.

And so I believed her when she said breastfeeding would come naturally. It didn't. I believed her when she said I'd know my own baby's cry from all the other babies in the hospital. I didn't. I believed her when she said my child would tell me all I needed to know about parenting once I was 'on the outside'. Well, unless there are hidden messages in all that random burping and farting, I don't think my baby was saying anything other than 'Who the hell are you?' and 'Is this all I have to work with?'

It's outrageous that hospitals and doctors and midwives can leave parents so ill-equipped for the tasks ahead. You won't find an antenatal class in the world that will tell you that you'll wake up one morning to a silent house, panic that your baby has died of SIDS but elect to deal with it WHEN YOU'RE FEELING MORE AWAKE. No textbook will tell you that. No textbook is honest and ordinary enough to make you see how parenthood will mess with the very wiring of your brain.

Rather, we are left with two old chestnuts: instinct and commonsense. Never mind that prior to bringing a child into the world, many of us didn't have enough commonsense to leave a nightclub before the ugly lights came on. In fact, most of us enter the world of parenting armed with little more than a few empty promises, a shaky resolve and a small person with a giant head. We have to learn the old-fashioned way: through mistakes, trial and error, and lashings of indefinable love.

Yes, in spite of everything you may read in parenting books and magazines, at the end of the day you'll simply have to wing it. We each have to pick up the ball and run in any direction we can. And if we manage to get away with any of it, we should consider it a bloody miracle.

Speaking of which, birth hurts a lot. Hurts like about four thousand ingrown toenails jammed in a car door. Despite that important fact, countless books and videos and midwives and smug mothers will tell you that birth is infinitely *more* miraculous when you manage it drug-free.

Silly me. I thought availing oneself of as many pain-relieving drugs as can be found in the average maternity hospital would be a clever approach to managing the improbable task of pushing a basketball out of a gumball dispenser. But it seems birth is as susceptible to fashion and social pressures as anything else.

And these days, natural childbirth is where it's at. It's hip, it's happening, it *hurts*.

In hospitals throughout the western world, prospective parents now eye epidurals as they might a second helping of dessert, boldly saying 'Thanks, but no'. They are (rightly) sceptical of the encroaching role of technology into what was once a solid afternoon's work in a spare cornfield. They look with suspicion upon impatient doctors and overworked midwives and are determined to reclaim control of all major bodily outgoings. They are staring down fear with a bucketful of essential oils and joining together in one mantra: 'I am woman, hear me exhale.'

Possibly the best thing about this philosophical shift back to managing sheer, unadulterated pain with little more than a wallet wedged between one's teeth and a wet towel is that it frees up more artificial pain-killers for those of us who really need them. I'm happy to admit that my pain threshold hovers somewhere between having a bandaid ripped off and getting a roller brush caught in my hair. I cross the road to avoid dentists. I need an oral anaesthetic to even contemplate a blood test. I once slapped an overzealous beautician mid-tweak and the thought of a Brazilian wax renders me foetal.

I also lack stamina. I've been known to walk out of standard-length movies because I simply can't concentrate for that long, my bum is numb, and my popcorn won't go the distance. Thus the very idea of an unassisted labour with no definitive end in sight is not only about as appealing as ironing a year's worth of pleated netball skirts; it's simply NOT AN OPTION.

Yes, I required a lot of drugs to cope with labour, yes, I asked for a take-home pack for later, and *yes*, I'm proud of it! And so should we all be!! Ladies, you'll be offered a dictionary of natural alternatives to chemical pain relief when next you find yourself staring down the barrel of a happy-gas nozzle. And good on you for even considering them (be sure to email me if you happen to hear of any yoga pose that numbs every part of one's body bar the head). But don't feel bad if you abandon them all after your 853rd contraction. After all, most of these alternative measures have been developed by men and most men need a week to recover after eighty minutes of footy.

I don't, for example, recommend that pregnant women rely solely upon any of the birthing 'comfort measures' advocated by international birthing expert Dr Michael Odent. Right off the bat, his suggestion that 'dimming the lights' in order to 'decrease neo-cortical activity' fails to recognise that when it comes to punching the person who got them into this position in the first place, women have the night-vision of a white pointer. Similarly, 'having the presence of a mother figure on hand' may not achieve anything remotely calming, unless of course she's armed with an uzi full of pethadine and isn't afraid to use it.

I do, however, agree with Dr Odent's overriding suggestion that a birthing woman should 'be free to follow her instincts'. And if your instincts are to stick with the guy in the lab coat earning $750 a jab, then, hey, knock yourself out.

Another emergent birthing fad that greatly worries me is the race to get out of hospital in record time.

'Seventy-three minutes!' screamed my friend Fiona about a colleague of hers who'd just given birth between school fund-raising meetings. 'That's a new record!'

'But that's ridiculous', I said. 'The drugs wouldn't have even worn off by then. She's probably wandering around stark naked in Westfield by now. Somebody should go and find that baby.'

Not for the first time I was left to wonder if I might be inhabiting a different plane of existence from my friends and fellow ovaried types. Don't these women realise that once you leave hospital with your new baby, they DON'T LET YOU BACK IN? No matter how much you knock on the front doors late at night and plead for a little more time? No matter how strongly you insist that you just need them to show you one more time how to attach correctly? God knows I tried to get back into hospital after having my first child, but those midwives were Nazis. 'You were in here for *six* days, Carrie,' they said. 'That's much longer than the average person and as much time as we're allowed to provide under hospital policy. We're happy to answer your questions, but only if you take your hand off the emergency button and back away slowly . . .'

Why the big rush to leave the druggy buzz and hype that envelops a busy maternity ward? Personally, I didn't even mind the urgent screams of other people's babies throughout the night (at least I *think* they were other people's babies), nor the happy madness of visiting hours. Mostly, though, I simply relished having all that expertise on tap. What's not to love about being surrounded by all-knowing midwives only too happy to tweak one's uncooperative nipple into place, or demystify meconium, or demonstrate how not to inadvertently drown a baby during its first bath? (Fellas, stick with me here.)

It's a crime that shrinking hospital budgets and nursing shortages have now led to a situation where too-short maternity stays are not only encouraged; they are applauded. Why are we paying all this tax and private health insurance if not to be able to afford ourselves a decent lie-down after the biggest physical effort of our lives?

Hospital stays should be like holidays: two days to settle in, two days to take full advantage of the facilities, and one day to squeeze a few pinched towels into your go-home bag.

A quick note on mothers' groups. Contrary to what hospital nurses will tell you, these groups are *not* helpful forums for sharing ideas, comparing notes and providing communal support. They are solely created for the ongoing exchange of beefed-up, bloody, bold and beautiful birth stories. So either you massage your birth story into some sort of impressive shape or you cross your fingers and commence earnest lying. It's a tough market. Today's stories are fresh and innovative; they incorporate loads of new technology and medical jargon and are savvy to shifts in popular thinking. Some months caesareans are all the rage; others it's vaginal breech births with an episiotomy twist. Birth partners are taking starring roles, tying complicated reef knots in umbilical cords and shedding puddles of tears.

So be advised to take a notebook into that delivery room, jot down a few anecdotes between contractions, and let's not be stingy with those melodramatic adjectives. And may the best moan win!

Healthy diet for new mums

For new mothers faced with the prospect of reclaiming their pre-baby body in time for menopause, most modern diets fall well short of realistic. Even the Clothesline Diet, widely applauded for its simplicity, does at the end of the day require a clothesline that isn't nailed to a fence or perennially swamped by wet nappies.

Should you or your partner ever find yourself up the duff, the following is a far more realistic diet and lifestyle guide for rediscovering your knees after birth. Feel free to stick it on the fridge when next you're reaching for the Chocolate Montes . . .

Breakfast:

Delay preparing anything to eat until the tenth or eleventh time you wake up. Hopefully by then it will be about 5 a.m. and a far more respectable hour to cook porridge.

Forget porridge. Throw a piece of bread in the toaster and expect to come back for it in about three hours.

While breastfeeding in your underwear, have a sneak peak through the window at all the pretty, toned people out for their morning walks. Ask yourself: do they *really* look that happy?

Lunch:

Consider a piping hot bowl of lentil soup and wholemeal croutons. Not that appealing, is it? And like you've got the preparation time anyway. Instead, eat whatever remains of last night's dinner and move it on through with the perennial staple, a Vegemite sambo.

Vacuum vigorously for one to two minutes.

When the baby is finally down for an afternoon sleep, grab a magazine and head for the loo. Enjoy this moment of nirvana. Read all about how the stars shed their kilos by gesturing wildly about yoga during interviews.

Feel a little guilty about the fact you're still wearing your pyjamas. Resolve to don clean trackie-daks and take the baby for a walk when they wake up.

Clean poo off sides of cot and bath soiled, crying baby. Take yesterday's washing out of the machine and throw in dryer while burping baby one-handed. Reconsider merits of walk. And of unprotected sex.

Discover toast in toaster from breakfast time. Enjoy.

Dinner:
Thrust screaming baby into arms of partner as he enters the door, then demand he also opens the Kan Tong jar before even thinking about removing his coat. Accept husband's offer to order pizza again. Rue that pizzas don't come with Frequent Flyer points.

Feed, change, burp, change, settle and change the baby before finally putting them to bed. Collapse into heap, noting that pyjamas are still feeling tight around middle. Check to see that you weren't perhaps harbouring twins.

Resolve to be more organised tomorrow, especially that bit about going for a walk. Remind yourself that celebrity mums only bounce back into shape because they adopt.

Make one final check on sleeping baby before hitting the sack. Note gorgeous little cheeks and contented purring sound. Give stretchmarks a grateful pat.

Nice work, if you can get over it

As outlined in the position vacant ad at the start of this chapter, parenting does come with its bonuses. For a start, there is that amazing period of unconditional love that immediately precedes a baby's discovery that nipples come in plastic varieties too. There's the day your child wins his or her first grand final in their chosen team sport—one of the best big-heart moments you'll ever feel. And there's the day they painstakingly select for you the best nursing home available for the price.

But it's not all beer and skittles. Without nobbling the federal government's earnest push that having several children is something other than a long and tedious journey of mundane and thankless self-sacrifice that no amount of comic satin boxer shorts on Father's Day could ever be worth, it's only right that this book sets the punters straight. In answer to a recent weekend newspaper article trumpeting the 'Eight surprising ways that kids make you healthy!', here is the mediocre lowdown:

1   **You will laugh more.** Actually, this is quite true. Parenthood does make you laugh uproariously and often. Unfortunately, it's usually at inopportune moments, like in the middle of a job interview when the prospective employer mentions that your position entails a lot of overtime and would that be a problem? No, of course not. I mean, ha ha. Ha ha ha HA HAAAAA!

2   **You'll get the best workout.** Also true to a degree. Certainly, in between chasing your tail, running out of excuses, skipping over the rude bits in videos, springing for other people's kids at McDonald's, and jumping to conclusions (*My lipstick is missing; I bet the loungeroom's sporting a new mural*), you could become one of the most active people you know.

3   **Your love will grow stronger.** Naturally. In the absence of sex, one tends to focus on the finer points of love, like waving to each other across the dinner table and buying milk on the way home without prompting.

4   **Kids enrich your life.** The subtext here is that kids introduce honesty, perspective and fun into a previously shallow life. With extra training, they'll even introduce you to the best-looking mum/dad at day care during a midweek grocery shop. And I'm certainly a happier person for that.

5 **Kids give you purpose.** Whether that comes before or after they give you headlice one can't be sure, but no doubt it's worth waiting for.

6 **Mothers have a decreased risk of breast cancer.** Apparently, if a woman has a child between the ages of twenty and thirty, her risk of breast cancer is halved. Could this be because her breasts are only half as big after weaning? Or simply because she doesn't have the spare time to grow a decent tumour?

7 **You will eat better.** Well, yes. Through the responsibility of parenting, you will learn to cook more vegetables. You will also learn to dispose of them quite efficiently at the end of each mealtime, and you will learn that kids, like adults, love a good pizza.

8 **Kids make you super-cool.** How this translates to being happier and healthier I'm not sure, but I have to admit that only through having a child did I learn that Britney Spears, Christina Aguilera and Jessica Simpson are actually three different people, and that fashion-wise, ground-in dirt is the new black. All of which should prove very handy one day when I least expect it.

Stay right where you are

Parenthood doesn't automatically cause advanced psychosis, provided that you simply stay home. But should you decide to leave your city of residence *with your children* ostensibly for the purposes of leisure, well, on your imploded head be it.

You see, travel is the very *antithesis* of parenthood. Travel is to parenthood what mosh pits are to the elderly—not a whole lot of fun unless you're heavily sedated. Travel might once have been a means of educating and liberating children beyond the class-room, but now we've got TV for that. I'm sorry, but you will never see a travel brochure depicting a happy smiling couple bounding along an empty foreign beach with two children, a stroller and a nappy bucket in tow. (If you do, alert the drug squad.)

It's just not *smart* to travel with kids, no matter how much it may seem wise and necessary to do so at the time. Case in point: the average baby takes eight hours to travel the fifteen centi-metres from womb to world. What does that tell you about how a two-thousand-kilometre-round car trip might go?

Children don't like being removed from their own environ-ment. Those that do like it so much they generally get lost within the first five minutes of arriving at a destination. I have friends who spent the first seven hours of their first overseas holiday attempting to locate their four-year-old at the airport. The poor child had done a runner, far from impressed that not only had her favourite teddy bear been left on the plane but also that her mother was no longer recognisable beneath layers of flowing sarong, a $2 sombrero and a ridiculous grin.

Kids are simply too young to understand that we adult types need holidays. Nor do they appreciate that we have little choice but to take them with us. ('No, kids, we didn't really think you'd enjoy a six-hour tour of the war memorial where your grand-father was buried but LIKE WE HAD A CHOICE?!')

It is often said that the best part of travel is in the journey, not the destination. But again, methinks whoever said this wouldn't know what a child looked like if it ran up and bit them on the leg. The truth of the matter for parents is that if you actually *can* get to your destination *with* children in tow and *without* losing your sanity, your luggage or any of said children,

then the destination is *everything*. It is, quite simply, nirvana. (You may even come to see a 'Kids' Club' as something other than a ready weapon.)

Because your options for simply Getting There range from the following:

◎ A *looong* car ride punctuated by interminable pee stops, random episodes of car sickness, 1482 games of I Spy that all begin with 'S' and stand for 'Sky', and a grumpy spouse who spends the trip reassessing their approach to contraception for the next twenty years.

◎ A plane trip that costs approximately a gazillion dollars and begins with you wearing your courtesy meal down your front and ends in a heated exchange with the guy in front of you about why on *earth* live children would ever be allowed on planes. (And while you suspect he's right, you will suddenly defend your screaming toddler with a passion bordering on insanity.)

◎ Train travel. As for car trips, but delete the pleasure of pee stops.

◎ Boats. Chaos, add water, stir vigorously.

Nope, my advice to new and would-be parents is simply to stay right where you are. Live vicariously through *Getaway*, salivate shamelessly over exotic brochures, steal your friends' travel albums if you must. But don't move an inch until your firstborn knows how to spell 'twinshare'.

A quick word on 'The Talk'

Every child at some point should be made to endure The Talk: those few carefully chosen sentences we use to explain to our offspring where they came from and what brand of absurdity is happening to their developing bodies. Modern parenting commentators like to suggest that The Talk, done carefully and honestly, can in fact prove a rewarding bonding experience for parent and child. This is *so* not true. The Talk *will* go badly for you, just as it did for thousands before you.

You will not bond with your child, nor will you impart anything greater than mutual embarrassment and disgust. Not only will you be forced to describe an activity that, minus dimmed lighting and a 'come hither' expression, must sound an awful lot like a fairly misguided game of Twister; you will also leave your children with little doubt that you engaged in this bizarre ritual on at least one occasion in the past.

Far preferable to The Talk is the 'Here, Read This' method of sexual education, in which a sufficiently ambiguous cartoon picture is worth a thousand words. This approach lets just enough information fall through the cracks so that no teenager could possibly approach sex with any sense of confidence or haste.

This was certainly the rationale favoured by my parents' generation. Not wanting to stumble over terms that sound like obscure casserole ingredients, mums like mine instead handed over *Where did I come from?* and instructed us to go forth and read.

There is nothing wrong with this approach. Although I did initially fear it was my parents' way of telling me I was adopted, I quickly came to realise that this was in fact the evidence I needed to prove they had once liked each other.

Whatever your chosen medium, whatever your timing and whichever pathetic excuse you choose to introduce this unnaturally earnest trans-generational conversation to your offspring, simply remember that it pays to approach The Talk much like The Act itself: minimal build-up, ambiguous penetration, zero follow-up and fleeting satisfaction. Any questions?

Parenthood finds its own level

If children came with adequate instructions, we wouldn't have to resort to ripping off other parents for the brilliantly ordinary tips they've ripped off other parents. Thankfully, though, the black-market of parenting nous (a high-stakes trading market for good ideas, product roadtests and public embarrassments) is in place to ensure we don't end up repeating *all* the same dumb mistakes our parents did. While it's impossible to distinguish the more experienced parents from the completely clueless ones, there's actually a lot you can learn from both breeds in a pinch.

For example, when the circumstances call for you to mind one little tacker while another little tacker becomes a potential traffic victim, it's imperative to identify any fellow parent type who can briefly mind the less endangered species. Look for someone who exhibits dark rings beginning around the eyes and radiating down to the knees, has leftover bits of Yowie toys dangling from their hair, and generally develops an unsightly twitch at the mention of new-season swimwear. On weekends you'll usually find bona fide parents moping about in the Weekly Releases section of the video store. (Real parents know they have as much chance of finishing a new release movie in one night as Posh Spice has of finishing a Best Of compilation). Furthermore, tried-and-true parents wear only drip-dry clothing, appear to enjoy their in-car music entertainment just a little too enthusiastically, and answer 'For chrissakes, no!' to most questions without even thinking.

More experienced parents tend to rise to the fore during times of crisis, having honed MacGyver-like skills from the challenges of changing nappies at crowded bus stops, producing well-balanced playgroup lunches from little more than an egg and a stick of celery, and creating award-winning fairy costumes with just a rubber band and two paddlepop sticks. Don't even try to compete with these people. Simply encourage your children to become close friends with theirs.

If you can't find any type of fellow parent when you need one, opt for the next best thing: an elderly woman in a hand-knitted cardie. Not too elderly, of course—she needs to be capable of holding your baby should you need to go wee-wees yourself while in a public toilet without stroller access—but just old enough that her smug expression says, 'Hey, I've made children who lived long enough to make other children, so you might want to listen up when I say I think your five-year-old could do with a good clip around the ears'.

You'll really need to rally the troops when your children are too old to still be parented by *Sesame Street*, because contrary to popular belief, the hardest years of parenting are not the first five. All those sleepless nights, toilet torture and demonic tantrums are simply preparing you for what lies ahead . . . SCHOOL.

See, school is hard because teachers are underpaid and they blame *you*. They want to bring your smug self undone with more notes and homework and special requests and sponsorship forms and book club orders and assignments than you ever thought possible. They want you to scratch your own eyes out trying to remember whether it was *today* that your child had to wear their formal uniform for school photos or whether in fact *this* was the day only a sports uniform would save your child from social ostracisation at the hands of the Netball Nazis.

As if school wasn't hard enough the first time you scraped through with scabbed knees and a tortured soul; school life as a parent is just one glaring error after another humiliating oversight. So chill out. Move your desk to the middle of the classroom and hook up with those parents around you who can form a neat, elite survival team for getting through the worst of it. Be sure to get yourself a:

◎ **Pajero Parent:** This is a mum or dad who spends ninety-five per cent of their waking hours in the car, happily ferrying not only their own children but yours and countless other strays from tennis to swimming to scouts to netball practice every afternoon and most weekends; and a

◎ **Secretary of the P&C:** This parent views the running of a school not unlike the machinations of a multinational corporation, complete with internal coups and overthrows of power. While none of this is of any real interest to you, it helps to know a P&C freak when you're unsure whether or not today is one of those ridiculous 'Student Free Days' or if your School Contribution Fund happens to be four hundred days late; and a

◎ **Don't-Mind-If-I-Do Parent:** Your friend at the bar. This person is not above smuggling a cask into carols by candlelight nor suggesting that a wine-tasting stall at the annual fete would be a ripper idea; and most importantly a

◎ **Fellow Imposter Parent:** Like you, this parent is muddling their way through school armed with very little information and a healthy dose of false bravado. This is someone with whom you can share many a mid-morning cappuccino, and laugh, about the time you completely outfitted your child in the uniform of a school eight suburbs away, and the day you unwittingly sent them to the library with a Victoria's Secret lingerie bag to bring home *The cat in the hat*.

The most beautifully ordinary lessons of parenthood . . . are those your children will teach you.

At the end of the day, the only things we adults can with any authority teach our children are: *Turn it off at the wall first* and *Don't pick it*. Manic little migraines though they are, children know just about all the important lessons about life that we adults subsequently allow work, money, relationships and success to comprehensively undo. In fact, if a pre-ten-year-old could spell mediocrity, they could have written this book. They've certainly got the whole 'life more ordinary' gig down pat. Take note . . .

◎ Children never say 'when'. Projectile vomiting is the only indication a little too much ice-cream may have been consumed.

◎ Parties represent a social nightmare for adults. Whether hosting one or going to one, there's so much food, wardrobe, music and conversation pressure to overcome before one can happily dance naked on a table and forget the whole debacle ever happened. Kids show up, fork over a present, eat like savages and refuse to go home until a lolly bag is forthcoming.

◎ When it comes to choosing a vocation, kids know it's all about the outfit. Forget the money and the company car, if it doesn't have a cape or a mask, it's just not worth the effort.

◎ Kids don't mourn the end of a friendship. You jump on my castle, I waste your teddy bear. It's that simple.

◎ Little kids love their parents unconditionally. Adults (and teens) blame their parents unconditionally.

◎ Little kids think success is making the swing go right over the top.

◎ Children think a twenty cent piece is a million dollars and a five dollar note is something to draw on.

◎ Children think every day can be a weekend if there's a park involved.

◎ Children only drag around as much 'baggage' as they can fit in a *Bob the Builder* backpack.

◎ Many adults spend decades working for the sort of bastard a kid would kick in the shins and leave for dust.

◎ A child's default setting is a smile. Wear the same expression as an adult and you're just a smug prick in need of knocking down a peg or two.

◎ Children recognise that the mixture somehow tastes better than the cake. Like life itself, what's the point in getting to the end if you can't lick the bowl along the way?

So the next time someone accuses you of childish behaviour, give yourself a little pat on the back and crack open the nearest bottle of Ice Magic. You're obviously doing something right.

Chapter 6

A short, mediocre guide to history

History is indeed little more than the register of the crimes, follies and misfortunes of mankind.
Edward Gibbon (1737–94), *Decline and fall of the Roman Empire*

Londoner John Evans, aged fifty-four, balanced ninety-six milk crates on his head without using his hands, for ten seconds. Earlier, he had balanced a Mini Cooper car on his head and also a ladder with a woman sitting on a bike at each end.

Lloyd Scott, aged forty-one, kitted out in a deep-sea diving suit, took six days, four hours, thirty minutes and fifty-six seconds to complete the Edinburgh Marathon in 2003. Thanks to a bout of food poisoning, this run surpassed his previous efforts of five days each for both the New York and London marathons.

In August 2003, Cuban cigar-maker Jose Castelar Cairo spent five days rolling a forty-five-foot-long stogy. (Oval Office interns are reportedly still wincing.)

Impersonator Kjell Henning Bjoernstad of Norway sang an uninterrupted medley of Elvis songs for twenty-six hours, four minutes and forty seconds in a bar in Oslo. 'It's now or never', he explained to weary onlookers.

Twenty-four-year-old Ma Lihua took seven weeks out of her happening social life to lay out 303 621 dominoes, stopping only to pick up the 10 000 that were knocked over by a rogue cockroach. Her completed work took just four minutes to knock down.

Swedish hottie Anders Mellert spent seventeen minutes and eight seconds in a sauna cranked up to 110 degrees Celsius.

And Mike Newman drove a super-charged Jaguar to a speed of 231 kilometres per hour at an aerodrome in York. The forty-one-year-old, who is also completely blind, said afterwards: 'I'm so happy. It really goes like the clappers.'

So what do all these delightful nutbags have in common? Quite obviously, they all wanted to *go down in history*. To be written into immortality and remembered always.

It's an odd, almost ironic, bent of humankind that sees us wish to be makers of history, especially in light of our otherwise fairly ambivalent attitude towards the past. Sure, we love to learn about it, but seldom do we learn *from* it, preferring instead to make our own sweet way forward, often repeating the same brand of mistakes that were themselves repeats of someone else's mistakes. As historian Julian Barnes so eloquently put it: 'History just burps, and we taste again that raw-onion sandwich it swallowed centuries ago.'

Yet documented history, itself a mediocre five-thousand-year effort at jotting down a few notes out of two million years worth of human existence, remains a revered record of people and events. We assume it to be full of the great and pivotal moments that have taken us from knuckle-scraping morons wielding clubs to beer-swilling idiots clutching mobile phones.

But it's not. It's really not. History is full of very ordinary, very mediocre people and events that, collectively and essentially, have woven together the colourful rug upon which we all now thrash about and occasionally recline.

Yes, history is mostly marvellous for its ordinariness. And in the spirit of such insight, and in the tradition of those mediocre scholars who only use the bits that fit their argument, this book proudly brings you the dramatically abridged, factually challenged, cynically illuminating 'Short, mediocre guide to history . . .'

Prehistoric man: the original late riser

Like a Tupperware party nightmare writ large, the earth waited four thousand and seven hundred million years for its first guests to arrive. Continents and oceans had formed, mountains had shaped themselves, even dinosaurs had briefly stuck their noses in, but it was all starting to seem for nought.

Finally, out of nowhere, the first hominids turned up for a squiz. With little else to amuse themselves, they began to mess around with their physical appearance, gradually enlarging their skulls and shrinking their oversized jaws ('Do my molars look big in this?').

At some point, between 1.5 million and four hundred thousand years ago, one member of this ancestral species elected to stand up, presumably to adjust himself. Happy with the new perspective this look afforded, he instructed his mates to do likewise and officially deemed it worthwhile to remain upright, if only to keep the monkeys off one's back.

Somehow, and many believe accidentally, these ancestors of modern man worked out how to make fire and presumably fashioned their own burns unit soon after. They lived in caves and also built rudimentary huts on large plains of land, possibly with a view to future subdivision.

Critically, it was his ability to make tools that separated early man from his animal friends. And this is also where we can first clearly observe his innate fondness for half-hearted stabs of effort.

EARLY MAN DISCOVERS FIRE

First up, a simple hand-axe was created by chipping away thick flakes from flint with bone or hard wood. Though it could barely cut through the air at an awkward cave party, this tool was deemed sharp enough to do the job for the next several hundred thousand years. And according to fossil records, not a single new idea or marginal improvement was thought up in the meantime. Man did not wish to bring on early fatigue by getting ahead of himself; early extinction be damned.

Ingeniously, and in the tradition of the many public servants he pre-dated, man waited until the evolution of the next species—our own *Homo sapiens sapiens* about fifty thousand years ago—to get around to fashioning a more efficient tool. And archaeological records reveal that he was indeed able to achieve a sharper edge on that piece of flint at around this time— a brilliantly mediocre show for a million or so years of really thinking about it.

But before such effort could become a bad habit—a catalyst for keeping the evolutionary ball rolling—man found distractions in the form of racial segregation and artistic expression. In terms of the former, man elected to spice things up a bit around the campsite by effectively dividing the species into distinct groups. Historically, there seems no obvious rationale for having done this apart from the possible prescient sense of emerging footy codes. Whatever the case, it wasn't long before insecurities and hatred took root, and everyone was so darn busy pointing out their differences and attacking each other in the dead of night that plans for sharper pieces of flint were perpetually relegated to the too-hard basket.

The other distraction, artistic expression, took its form in cave markings. Man found he was able to 'freeze' part of his environment long enough to really think about it. In fact, sometimes he thought so long and hard about it that he forgot to hunt and eat, hence the early origins of the term 'starving artist'.

But apart from plotting racial genocide and smearing clay on the walls, man did very little for a good thirty thousand years or so. Many early historians assumed that the prehistoric people who lived by hunting animals and gathering plants were faced with a constant threat of starvation and therefore spent all day and most of the night searching for food. In actual fact, early man gave himself an abundance of leisure time and preferred a high mortality rate over a sweaty brow any day of the week.

Only one in ten people at this time would have lived to the age of forty, but the intervening years were spent sleeping, playing games and clearing bellybutton lint. Indeed, recent studies of early Kalahari bushmen and Australian Aborigines showed that early man probably only worked a few hours each day—thirty hours a week tops—and in all likelihood spent the rest of the day wondering why the hell he was here.

But he was 'throwing the leg over', of course. Women of this time were perennially pregnant or breastfeeding—even then, 'no' apparently meant 'yes'. Their daily life was divided between tending to hungry children, nursing the community's diseased and picking up after their husbands.

Men, meanwhile, had a few problems of their own, especially after they finally progressed from that dodgy piece of flint to the fashioning of a crude harpoon. Hunting expeditions became the most frequent cause of human death, less so the death of animals, and the only thing that may well have kept us going at this point was the still universal appeal of 'one more for the road'.

Fortunately, about fifteen thousand years ago, the earth's climate started to improve (a change no doubt missed by forecasters at the time), thus making it a slightly more hospitable place to hang out. Temperatures rose, ice sheets melted away, and it was probably around this time that man experimented with his first backyard water feature.

By about 8000 BC, man's development became more rapid as little discoveries begat new ones. Early attempts at domesticating plants and animals eventually yielded success, and man the hunter gradually become man the farmer. This new age, the so-called Neolithic Revolution, became arguably the most important and far-reaching of all revolutions right up until the advent of PubTAB.

Growing more than one's family needed gave rise to the possibility of trade (not to mention long weekends and Christmas bonuses). And those people who didn't grow things to barter and sell went ahead and made items themselves: pottery, necklaces, carvings and charcoal portraits. Thankfully, even back then, plenty of people were only too willing to buy useless homemade crap at market stalls.

A more secure food supply and better nutrition all 'round soon led to a population explosion. Communities grew and spread, reaching out to almost every inhabitable corner of the earth. Women, still barefoot and pregnant, created kitchen areas within their homes and busied themselves making food, clothing and rods for their own backs.

The discovery of metal and metalwork, most likely around eight thousand years ago by a cluey group of craftsmen in western Asia, finally dragged man out of the Stone Age and made way for the prospect of an industrial revolution.

Having created so much new work for himself, and so many new questions at the same time, man finally laid claim to that which was rightfully his: a decent lie-down.

Little engines that could

Contrary to popular belief, the world doesn't owe its civilised existence to Christopher Columbus and a handful of great Americans with dreams and moonsuits. In fact, America barely rates a mention in the critical few thousand years that saw the world create a semblance of order from what had previously been a bit of a dog's breakfast.

Indeed, no irresponsibly potted history of the world would be complete without a quick round of hearty backslaps for those cultural groupings who, in simply going about their daily business and often through sheer slackness, established basic templates of living for civilisation today. In no particular order, the nominees are:

The Semites (3000 BC– 135 AD): Originators of the Keep It Simple Stupid (or KISS) principle, the Semites who settled along the eastern shores of the Mediterranean some five thousand years ago were the first to cull god numbers, which had frankly got out of control. On the suggestion of the Hebrews, they declared the future worship of one god only, thus keeping prayer times more manageable and focused. Millions of Christians, Jews and countless other religious followers around the world are still grateful for this insightful clearing of the decks.

Ancient Greece (800–30 BC): Although their achievements in the arts, science, building and philosophy shaped the culture of the entire western world, it is perhaps for their attitude that we should be most thankful to the ancient Greeks. 'Nothing in excess'—their simple inscription on the now famous shrine at Delphi—urges moderation in all things, balance in one's endeavours and, if you'll indulge me the interpretation, the pursuit of a certain ordinariness to life. Dubious about the quality of life after death, the Greeks encouraged the importance of life *now*: of days in the sun, of wine o'clock, of satisfaction over sacrifice. 'Come on, come on, get happy!' could well have been their theme song. God love 'em.

Nothing in excess.
The ancient, awesome
Greeks (circa 500 BC)

Rome (753 BC–476 AD): The Romans were pretty bloody full of themselves by the end of their five hundred years or so of global domination. The world's first true party-poopers, their penchant for overachievement destabilised the rickety pillars of mediocrity established by more fun-loving empires before them, such as Greece and Mesopotamia.

Thankfully, though, we have at least some worthwhile legacies of Rome's testosterone-fuelled reign, namely a powerful judicial system, republican-based systems of government, caesar salads and Russell Crowe in a tunic.

Mediocrity Hall of Fame
Member: Archimedes (290-212BC)

Though exceptionally gifted in the fields of mathematics and logic, Archimedes seemed destined to be remembered for anything but. His most astonishing discovery—that the amount of water an object displaced was a direct measure of the object's volume—became known more for the style of its revelation than its relevance: a dripping wet Archimedes leaping from the bath and running tackle-happy to the King of Syracuse with the cry of 'Eureka! I've found it!' ('What? The plug?' mused the King.)

Notwithstanding such gonadic derring-do, Archimedes was entrusted with the development of 'engines of war' to defend Syracuse from the invading Romans. He became so immersed in his work that he didn't even notice a dagger-toting Roman at his side one morning.

'Bugger off,' said Archimedes, 'I'm working'.

Reportedly, the amount of blood displaced was a direct measure of the dagger's volume.

And we have Mediocrity Hall Of Fame contenders like Augustus, the adopted son of Julius Caesar, who claimed his inheritance after Caesar's assassination in 44 BC. Expected by many to complete Caesar's ultimate plan—the conquering of Britain, land of opportunity—Augustus decided he frankly couldn't be bothered.

Oh and there's Claudius (10 BC–54 AD), who famously hid in the Roman palace to avoid taking over the top job after Caligula was assassinated. Alas, he was found behind a large pot plant and crowned the new emperor of Rome. Eventually bowing to peer pressure, Claudius also became a soldier and, oh *okay* then, invaded Britain. But his heart wasn't in it and he could barely convince himself of his battle plans, let alone the Senate. Before long, Claudius became one of the most hated—and certainly misunderstood—shirkers in Rome. In the end, his fourth wife Agrippina narrowly beat out all his would-be assassins. If only they'd let him have a desk job like he'd wanted.

India (from 2400 BC): Australia reveres its many 'little battlers', but we've got nothing on the Indians. Possibly the most ancient civilisation in the world, India has calmly endured more invasions, more turmoil and more external pressure from the rise and fall of empires around them than any other civilisation. This is perhaps thanks to Buddha, their much-worshipped sedentary diety, whose fondness for sitting on his backside and doing bugger-all has inspired one of the most popular and least messy of all religious philosophies.

In fact, Buddhism is now officially the fastest growing religion in Australia, according to the latest census figures, and it's probably worth considering why. There has to be more than coincidence to the fact that Buddhism's Four Noble Truths find many parallels with Australia's admirably lackadaisical ways—and indeed with the premise of this book.

For a start, Buddhism's First Noble Truth concedes that life is full of suffering. It follows that it's only sensible to lower one's expectations about fairness, fortune and success in life, and to instead assume a safe and comfortable sitting position whenever possible.

By extension, the Second Noble Truth attributes much of life's suffering to craving and aversion. It states that getting what you want in life doesn't guarantee happiness, so it makes more sense to give up the struggle, modify your wants and wait for a few of them to float by in the slipstream.

The Third Noble Truth advocates that true happiness becomes more likely when we learn to live each day at a time and upon its own merits. In other words, don't dwell on the past and don't stress out about the future. In turn, if today looks dodgy, call in sick, flick on Bert and bring your 6 p.m. drinkypoo forward to 1 p.m.

The Fourth and final Noble Truth is divided into the Noble 8-Fold Path, a moral code that is further defined by the five Buddhist Precepts. Frankly, it's all getting a bit spreadsheety now, so let's move on.

Stuck in the Middle Ages

This brings us neatly enough to western civilization; a complex animal with its roots in the past, its eye on the future and its hand usually in the till.

Picking up the story from the start of the so-called Middle Ages, about five hundred years after Christ was nailed on a bum rap, we find Europe still dazed and confused after the timely fall of the party-pooping Roman Empire of tryhards. While barbarian kings tried valiantly to rebuild their beloved Rome (it's amazing what you can do with a team of tradesmen, a major hardware sponsor and two solid days), the Christian church quickly emerged as a more powerful global entity.

No doubt unwittingly, the Pope and his many fashion-challenged bishops and clergy convinced medieval Europe to finally shed the psychological shackles of slavery and to embrace an easier—albeit still class-impoverished—way of life. By preaching that every man and woman was regarded as a unique creation of God, the slave societies of ancient Rome, Greece and Egypt were soon looked upon as evil. Instead, people came to think of their labour as something worth selling and, more importantly, something to be compensated for with a full and active social life.

'Work hard, play harder', became the unofficial motto of the Middle Ages' peasant society. And of course what followed became an important template for life today, an antidote to the unhealthy success-at-all-costs of masters, lords and team leaders . . . the era of the pub.

Work hard, play harder.
unofficial motto,
Middle Ages' peasants

Yes, we have the Middle Ages to thank for the liberating salvation of a hard-won ale or six at the end of the day. Particularly as feudalism started to falter, people would spend increasingly more of their extra time and money in local taverns—a pastime that pleased everyone except the church. In fact, it wasn't until the modern advent of online gaming in pubs that priests too realised what all the fuss was about, signed up for Keno and quit banging on about the evils of the demon drink.

The Middle Ages tavern was where it was at. It was where you could drink, play cards, dice and 'mini-archery' (apparently it was conducted indoors like darts); and outside, in the dingy alley, you could generally find a makeshift ten-pin game in full swing. (Even back then, 'bowling alleys' made heroes out of men who were useless at all other sports.)

With the average medieval peasant usually carking it by the age of twenty-seven, it's not hard to see why this fun-loving lifestyle, this rejection of blind ambition in favour of getting blind, was so popular. Eat, drink and be merry, peoples, for tomorrow we may die!

At the same time, people didn't *hate* work; it was simply something they had to do. Another tenet of mediocrity for which we have the Middle Ages to thank is the belief that there is no shame in a simple working-class existence. Whereas previous civilisations such as Mandarin-ruled China believed menial work was a badge of shame, medieval Europe took pride in the fact that it worked; that it had earned another night in the tavern. Indeed, if we accept many historians' categorisation of medieval society as being 'those who fight, those who work, and those who pray', most hard-living peasants reckoned they'd cornered the best part of the triangle.

Away from work and the pubs, the home life of your average Middle Ages family also instilled principles of simplicity and ordinariness that generations today have carried through. In short, many were lazy-bastard homekeepers who would much rather hear about other people's renovation stories than hammer in a single nail themselves.

And why should they? In those days, shoddy building materials meant that houses only lasted thirty years at best, so it would hardly be worth locating the Allen key to fix up that fallen shelving unit, would it? Indeed, historical records show that even though the weather was freezing most of the time, medieval homeowners couldn't be bothered building fireplaces that would only be around for thirty years tops. Instead, they dug a hole in the floor and surrounded it with rocks to make a permanent fire pit. The kiddies must have loved it.

Naturally, as a result of this practice, homes were permanently filled with smoke, as were the clothes worn by peasant families. Ingeniously, this was a good thing, because peasants couldn't be bothered changing their outer garments during winter (they would literally stitch themselves inside them until the sun came out) and the woodfired ambience of your average feral Middle Ages home had a deodorising effect on its inhabitants' clothes. Interestingly, many bachelors and divorced men today achieve a similar effect by always keeping their fetid pile of bathroom-floor cast-offs as close as possible to the aromatic blue tablet in the loo.

Like their clothes, the tools and utensils that Middle Agers used were generally fashioned at home with a minimum of effort and maximum haste. For example, rather than carving spoons and forks out of wood, most families chose utensils shaped out of cow horn because, as one historical writer noted, 'a little licking

replaced the need for washing up'. (Similarly, surveys of home-owners today rate the inclusion of a dishwasher as being more important than a roof or load-bearing walls.)

But far be it for me to suggest that Middle Ages folk were dirty, smelly buggers. On the contrary, historical diaries show that communal bathing rated highly on the social agenda. Public baths or 'stews' as they came to be known, were so much fun that even wealthy castle types envied them, rightly suspecting that all the privately enjoyed perfumed rosewater in the world couldn't make up for the hilarity of working out which bum was making all those porridge-smelling bubbles.

It's an oversight that today's makers of the classic Leisure Suit Larry video game haven't released a Middle Ages edition. This

Mediocrity Hall of Fame

Member: William The Conqueror (1028-87)

Sometimes death has the last laugh. Though he would've liked to have been remembered for his violent marauding and ruthless quashing of rebellions, William The Conqueror instead left mourners with the ill wind of his foul body odour.

A big man, Will's leisure suit of choice—full body armour—fermented frightful flesh fumes that turned his funeral into a farce. His body went mouldy very quickly and two undertakers actually caught a fever from William's corpse and died.

To add further folly to proceedings, a fire broke out adjacent to William's monastery tomb just as he was about to be buried and mourners had little choice but to abandon the funeral and fight the fire.

When things resumed, it was discovered that William's large rotting frame was too big for the stone tomb that had been created for him. However, rather than find an alternative on short notice (and endure that smell for any longer), the funeral attendants simply jammed the body in, causing various bits to fall off in the process. Nice.

surely was the era when man felt justified in balancing life's inherent hardship with as much rest and relaxation as possible. Medieval Europeans even bastardised time itself to make the most of visiting festivals, plays, seasonal celebrations such as Midsummer, and of course the prelude to modern reality TV—the bloody medieval tournament. When a man said he was going out for 'an hour or so', it could have meant anything from sixty to one hundred and fifty minutes or more because in the early Middle Ages at least, people decided that summer hours should be longer than winter ones. You know . . . just because. (Sadly, by the end of the 1300s, mechanical clocks had arrived to shatter their delusion.)

Although the world at this time didn't think of itself as middle-aged (and who ever does?), it most certainly was. Accordingly, it was more than due for a mid-life crisis. After almost a thousand years of relative stability afforded by the steadying influence of Christianity and the slightly less steadying influence of piss and bad manners, people were starting to scratch their paunches, stare off into space and ask 'Is this all there is?'.

Indeed, it was all fun and games until someone loosed a 'why?'

Renaissance man: Show me the money!

And so Europe finally shed its daggy middle-aged tunic and whipped on a pair of adventure pants, heralding the start of what became known as the Renaissance period. In every field of endeavour—philosophy, science, art, fashion, exploration, etc.— Renaissance men challenged accepted ideas (except the ones about women having to clean up after them) and sought to broaden their horizons. It was, in Keating terms, the revolution we had to have.

In many ways, the onset of the Renaissance was mankind's first go at a self-help movement. Life had started to fall into a predictable pattern of work, play, eat, die of bubonic plague—and many mistook this for a rut. They decided there had to be more to this existence gig and enthusiastically set about whipping everyone into a frenzy of hope and possibility. In town squares,

Anthony Robbins types started preaching that 'The future is in our hands!' . . . provided it all went through their hands first.

Of course, today's more illuminated person knows that life pretty much does fall into a predictable pattern and that too much inspiration and too many possibilities are simply traps for the unwary. But you have to remember that many of these Middle Agers had been drunk for thirty years and some had only just had their first set of decomposing clothes prised off.

Although commonsense had long told them that the earth was as flat as a papal knock-knock joke and that if one walked far enough across it, one would inevitably fall off, Renaissance adventurers like Christopher Columbus fell over themselves to disprove such alleged truths. Similar 'how big is your penis' competitions sprang up all over Europe. Nicolaus Copernicus raced to prove that the earth wasn't actually the centre of the universe, and artists continuously outdid each other in their efforts to replace antiquated artistic styles with more accurate depictions of contemporary life. Many didn't know art, but they knew what they liked.

The place was buzzing, man. Merchants backed expensive and experimental trade expeditions to distant lands, and quickly declared themselves specialists in finance and insurance. Mum-and-dad investors lost their life savings to strike-it-rich con men, who in turn justified their dishonesty by believing they were above a common existence and had the fridge magnet-style affirmations to prove it.

More money flying about the place meant more to spend on leisure, however in the absence of poker machines, many families sought to direct their wealth towards home improvements, spurring demand for extra arts, crafts and tacky knick-knacks. Tonia Todman's ancestors knitted themselves

Mediocrity Hall of Fame

Member: Christopher Columbus (1451-1506)

Known to generations of school children as the man who discovered America, Columbus was in fact a hopeless driver who had been trying to find his way west to the Orient when he hit the 'new world' in 1492. So convinced was he that he'd landed at the Indies that Columbus even called the natives he found there 'Indians'.

Returning to Spain a hero, Columbus was made 'Viceroy of the Indies' and soon commanded an even larger voyage. He reported back that he was discovering even more uncharted territory leading to the elusive Orient, but his financiers began to suspect, quite rightly, that Columbus was somewhere very different entirely.

Poor organisation meant that subsequent voyages resulted in humiliation and defeat, and finally Columbus was stripped of his Viceroy title. He died a disappointed man, completely unaware that the country he had stumbled upon would one day consider him a founding hero and name a Big Mac in his honour.

stupid and homewares sellers began to realise that a ten cent curtain ring could also be marketed as a $10 napkin ring within a set of six. Interestingly, this early misconception of renovation being a fun application of time and money has had a second resurgence in modern times.

Here was an era where one could really be a jack of all trades and master of none. Even da Vinci took his painting hand to sculpting, anatomy, engineering, maths, philosophy, botany and an early form of pilates. He wasn't necessarily much chop at them all, but this was a time when being even mediocre at a lot of things made you somewhat of a star. By comparison, today you can be mediocre at one thing and still be a star—take a bow Anna Kournikova, Mark Philippoussis, Keanu Reeves, Dannii Minogue, Eddie Maguire and the entire cast of *Home & Away*.

Significantly, it wasn't productivity and global advancement that were inspiring our go-get-em Renaissance man. No, it was generally the sheer prospect of personal fame. That, and a fat wad of cash. It was an age of rampant individualism, of there being no 'I' in teamwork, of God helping those who helped themselves. In a rough-hewn nutshell, it was the historic justification for today's obsession with reality TV. For as much as man is inherently lazy, he is also inherently self-obsessed. Reality TV is the perfect convergence of these two innate traits and it shouldn't surprise anyone that it has come to dominate the culture of the early twenty-first century.

Even Martin Luther, reformer of Christianity during the Renaissance period, prophetically saw that greater exposure for his message lay in 'dumbing it down' for the masses and so replaced traditional Latin church services with more real-to-life, native-tongue versions involving role play and amateur drama. He stopped short of allowing congregation members to vote off preachers who were becoming boring.

But perhaps nowhere was the nascent power of mediocrity more apparent during this time than within royal circles. Then, as now, being born into royalty was an open cheque for a lifetime of fame and power; a ticket to success and glory stamped with DNA.

Enter the Hapsburgs—the rulers of Austria, Bohemia and Hungary and countless lands between. Delusion and laziness

Mediocrity Hall of Fame
Member: Anne Boleyn (1504-36)

Plenty of women throughout history have married duds, but perhaps none with less of an excuse than Anne Boleyn, the last of Henry VIII's wives to be beheaded. Only Larry Fortensky, fifty-sixth husband of Elizabeth Taylor, had more dubious evidence stacked against him. How could Anne have thought her neck was any less loppable than those who had gone before her? Especially when one considers the volatile circumstances in which she married the short-tempered king.

After stealing Henry from Catherine of Aragon, Anne talked him into a 'secret' wedding—so secret that only the whole of England knew about it. No sooner had the confetti landed than Henry characteristically lost interest. By the time Anne delivered baby Elizabeth, who clearly lacked a set of crown jewels, the king was almost ropeable.

Anne soon came through with a boy, but tragically the baby was stillborn, and Henry promptly rode off in the direction of a pub. The next day Henry had Anne arrested, accusing her of adultery with her own brother and four commoners. Though Anne made an excellent case in her defense, saying that it would have been difficult to procure so much sex while still distraught and haemorrhaging, the lack of mobile phone records in those days meant that Anne ultimately lost her head. Like, hullo, *that* wasn't going to happen.

found perfect synergy in this mediocre family of misfits, who were so convinced they belonged to a superior brand of humankind that they didn't see reason nor bother in sleeping outside of it. The Hapsburgs were hopeless inbreds, at first deliberately and then just conveniently. They didn't even stop inbreeding when it became obvious that all their kissin' cousins' action had rendered their gene pool virtually unswimmable. The 'Hapsburg lip', an unsightly physical deviation, became increasingly more obvious with each generation, eventually producing guys like Charles II (King of Spain from 1665 to 1700), whose jaw was so deformed by the absurd structure of his mouth that he physically couldn't chew his food. He was also, truth be known, mentally retarded and impotent, the latter being nature's way of saying 'Enough with the family-only barbecues already!'

Of course, the Hapsburgs were nothing new in the tradition of European royal inbreeding. Romantic laziness and self-delusion were similarly evident in the big noses of the Bourbons and today in the wing-nut ears of the Windsors. Yes, inbreeding may well be its own punishment, but no historian could argue that it has held back a single royal dynasty from pursuing its own dubious ends. When it comes to the application of pure mediocrity, royalty is life's crowning glory.

And so as we come to the end of this Renaissance period, we see a world newly obsessed with itself and with what everyone else thinks about itself. Even wars of this time came to be about personal glory, not just land. Victory was triumph over another's mind, not just their home. The planet was behaving like a giant erection and it was almost two hundred years before it felt the tap of a cold spoon.

Don't start the revolutions without me!

Upon the insistence of philosophers (history's version of jaded radio jocks and newspaper columnists), Renaissance man decided to have a long, hard think about himself and his to-hell-with-the-consequences approach to life. A spate of scientific discoveries in the early seventeenth century both vindicated the philosophers' call and led to the growing assertion that life wasn't such a big mystery after all. Basic formulas and reasoning could, it seemed, explain just about everything to do with life and the universe (except for the existence of cats).

This more cerebral period in world history became known as the Enlightenment. In today's terms, it was the equivalent of a thinktank—the shifting of established paradigms through the application of fresh perspectives and outside-the-square rationalisation harnessing universal synergies. Or wankfests, as I like to think of them.

Then as now, over-intellectualising relatively simple concepts proved an alluring pastime and one that seemed to suck in a lot of punters. Rationalists like French philosopher René Descartes, for example, did away with all previous thinking and decided to start again at the beginning by identifying anything in life that couldn't be disproven. One of his most noted discoveries was that it is man's mind that does all the thinking (not, say, his elbow) and that this fact alone proves we exist. 'I think, therefore I am', he boldly announced to the world, a statement right up there with today's *Who moved my cheese?* in terms of its cerebral magnitude. If addictive little mints had been invented back in the 1700s, this would almost certainly have prompted the first corporate retreat.

Importantly, man had always had the capacity for profound analytical thought, he just hadn't stopped thinking about sex long enough to achieve it. The Enlightenment finally gave him the chance to exercise a different body organ. Indicatively, brainiacs like Isaac Newton emerged at this time to apply complicated logic

to simple phenomena. For example, after observing that even the ugliest of his friends usually managed to pull on a Friday night, he surmised that everything in the world had a mutual attraction for everything else. Bang. Law of Universal Gravitation.

But while all this cerebral postulating was going on, an undertow of social unrest was gathering strength. Towns had become overcrowded and poverty-stricken, farmers' families were starving to death, civil wars raged, illiteracy was rife, and most people died before the age of thirty-five. It may have been an Age of Reason, but the people were reasonably peeved. The only thing for it was to have a revolution.

Mediocrity seldom attracts the credit for history's most dramatic revolutions, yet it is almost always a person or act of less than impressive calibre that finally inspires people to consider the inconvenient hassle of bloody revolt. This was certainly the case with the French Revolution, arguably the most inspiring and influential of all revolutions, which transformed the running of that country and many others in its wake during the years 1789–99. By contrast, England's 'Glorious (and Bloodless)' Revolution of 1688 was, well, just that, and the American Revolution of 1775–83 talked itself up as being a saviour of civil liberties but failed to abolish slavery for at least another seventy years.

No, the French Revolution was as impressive as it was messy—a lot like the dimwit who inspired it: one Louis XVI. Louis, through his dubious intellect and economic bumbling, contributed greatly to a reversal of public trust in royal supremacy. Waltzing about the Versailles palace he'd taken forty-seven years to complete (much of which was spent chasing tradesmen's quotes), Louis managed to squander his country's entire piggybank, borrowing increasing amounts of money just to pay off the interest on his original debts. Besides himself and shopping-mad wife Marie-Antoinette, much of Louis' financial focus had been on helping America in its War of Independence from Britain—a fact that adds a certain ironic twist to the two nations' testy relationship today.

Taxed beyond belief, the French had begun to suspect that kings weren't beings appointed by God but were in fact little more than tossers in tiaras who couldn't make a profit selling warm beer to Irishmen. Frustrated and incredulous, they stormed the Bastille and set in train the most bitter and comprehensive revolution the world has ever seen (prior to the switch from Beta to VHS). The French Revolution saw hundreds of its aristocratic big nobs die by the guillotine (the very instrument they'd invented for criminals), and everywhere people started to question the power bases that had shaped their nations to date.

Of course, for those who weren't overly perturbed by any of the current power bases, it was simply a great time to embrace chaos, kick up the heels and try one's hand at various instruments of torture. Celebrity knitter Madame de Farge clickety-clacked out a fine line in post-revolutionary cardies for the inevitable after-bloodbath celebrations.

France's bloody rampage inspired a wave of revolution-style fever the world over. For a while there, everyone who was anyone was having one. Thankfully, history has always managed to guide talentless gits into positions of power so there has always been sufficient cause for disgruntled masses to topple governments. They're so much more efficient at it than opposition parties.

One of the most appealing aspects about war and revolution is their capacity to take the focus off the banality of everyday life. Suddenly the world is a more interesting place, even if you're not personally contributing one iota of effort to the melee. Every-day work commitments and the notion of progress seem to fall by the wayside, and it's perhaps for this reason that for the better part of the eighteenth century, very little in the way of mechanical innovation or progress took place. Horses and water were still the primary sources of power, roads were non-existent, all beer was home-brewed and mobile phone coverage was appalling.

Once the fighting died down, however, people with ideas and ideas awaiting people had the breathing space to bear fruit. An age of invention and discovery was about to take place, albeit with varying degrees of success and healthy dollops of mediocrity thrown in for good measure.

Revenge of the nerds

Edmund Cartwright (1743–1823)

Inventor Cartwright is historic proof that when one flukes a brilliant discovery, it pays to rest on one's laurels. Not content that he had saved the life of a boy dying of putrid fever by smearing a tub of yeast all over his body, the self-described 'ideas man' set about inventing a weaving machine. Unfortunately, his complete lack of knowledge about industry, patents, industrial relations and business law meant that Cartwright's weaving machine factories became the scorn of the community and the target for arsonists. People liked his steam engine idea even less. Unperturbed, Cartwright set about inventing a system of interlocking bricks and later an incombustible floor made entirely of fired clay. They collapsed and shattered respectively, though unfortunately his resolve did not. Cartwright continued to toil on his plans to build a steam-powered boat, but ultimately failed to follow through. Perhaps it's just as well Cartwright's last brilliant idea didn't reach fruition before his death. An engine fired by gunpowder was only ever going to end in tears.

Charles Babbage (1791–1871)

For all his natural mathematical wizardry and foresight, Charles Babbage seemed destined for mediocrity, at least while he insisted on breathing. His planned invention of the 'Difference Engine', a machine that could perform mathematical calculations to twenty decimal places and would effectively serve as the forerunner to the modern digital computer, was dogged by years of fighting about the ownership of his tools and the machine itself. After more than a decade of problems, government funding for his 'flights of fancy' dried up, and over time Babbage became an increasingly eccentric and depressed figure who believed that buskers were out to steal his soul. His move to enact a parliamentary act banning street musicians resulted in him becoming so unpopular that people actually threw dead cats at him in the street.

Following his death in 1871, Babbage's mathematical ideas were largely dismissed and his unpublished notes went underground. Exactly one hundred and twenty years later, someone unearthed them and set about building the 'Difference Engine' exactly to Babbage's specifications. It proved accurate to thirty-one decimal places.

Alexander Graham Bell (1847–1922)

From the moment he sacrificed the family cat in order to observe the inner workings of the vocal cords, young Alex Bell showed he would stop at nothing to achieve his ultimate life goal: the transmitting of speech along a wire. After years of intense research and false attempts, by 1875 he had finally developed the prototype of a simple receiver and rushed to patent his achievement. Although most history books don't show it, Bell had in fact been beaten to the punch four years earlier by Italian immigrant Antonio Meucci. However, as Meucci was too poor to afford the patent and Alex had buckets of family dosh, the credit struck Bell.

While he'd also been working on the idea of a telephone for some time, Bell's big breakthrough happened by sheer accident. When his colleague Watson was adjusting one of Bell's receivers one day, Alex heard the sound coming out of the other receiver—even though the transmitter had been turned off! This, he figured, meant that not only did electricity produce sound, but sound in turn produced electricity. He rushed to acquire a patent, beating his closest rival by just two hours.

Bell quickly became a very rich man, thanks mostly to soaring stocks in the Bell Telephone Company. But success had its way with his ego and soon there was nothing Bell thought he couldn't invent. Most interesting was his idea of developing sheep with extra nipples. He was convinced these sheep would give birth to more lambs, and spent years building giant sheep villages and counting sheep nipples well into the wee hours. Eventually the US State Department rang through the sad news: extra nipples were not linked with extra lambs. It wasn't long before a dejected Bell hung up.

Alfred Nobel (1833–96)

Fame and fortune never bought Alfred Nobel the happiness he desired. He rued his great invention, dynamite, for its ability to cause harm, and hid from the attention that people everywhere wanted to lavish upon him. But out of what Alfred might have considered a mediocre discovery from a mediocre scholar emerged a powerful legacy of honour and achievement that will continue to endure for generations to come: the Nobel prize. Upon his death bed, Nobel seriously peeved his relatives when he declared that instead of leaving his millions to them, he wished to leave them to humanity. By his decree, a portion of his fortune would each year accompany a medal awarded to people whose outstanding work promised to bring about the betterment of mankind. There would be three medals: one for discoveries in medicine and science, one for literature, and one for a person whose work had done most to bring about peace and harmony between nations. It was a world-changing idea from a sad and lonely man who'd wished he'd kept his biggest invention to himself. Belated success through (self-perceived) mediocrity . . . Alfred Nobel, rest in peace.

Anonymous (1896)

It is cruel indeed that history has failed to record the name of the man or woman who lodged US Patent No. 560 351 for the mechanical 'Dimple Drill'. Like all great mediocre ideas, this one derived from the combination of a simple observation and an even simpler question: namely, dimples look nice and, hey, if you're not born with them, is there any way you can make them?

The Dimple Drill had a rounded tip made of ivory or marble which, when gently 'drilled' into the desired spot for a dimple, would gradually encourage the skin to comply. Yup. It could also, the patent application insists, 'nurture and maintain existing dimples'. Why this cracker never reached manufacturing stage remains a mystery, but it just goes to show that the US Patent Office has always been an open-minded and accommodating lot, and that ideas only become stupid ideas when their creator fails to follow through. Here are a few other cases in point.

◎ **The Car Bib** (US Patent 4 878 513, issued 1980): For the driver that needs to eat on the go, 'The Car Bib' would catch the fries and mayonnaise that might otherwise compromise your next sales pitch. Why have we not seen this little gem in shops?

◎ **Cry No More** (US Patent 6 860 649, issued 2000): This strap-on pacifier will teach those no-good dribbling infants not to spit the dummy. Just watch them try to unhook the looping security straps affixed to their ears.

◎ **Extreme Comb Over** (US Patent 4 022 227, issued 1975): Just as no man expects to go bald, he also can't be expected to know how best to arrange what little hair might remain. The 'Extreme Comb Over' is a patented three-section styling technique that dictates how a man should ideally achieve 'the Swoop'.

◎ **Fingertip Toothbrush** (US Patent 5 875 513, issued 1999): This is actually really cool! How many times have you been stuck somewhere without your toothbrush and been forced to do the inelegant paste-on-pinky routine? This idea harnesses the nerve endings in one's finger and combines them with a weird rubbery device you'd be hard-pressed explaining to a new partner. It even has a circular bit at the base of the contraption that catches all your saliva.

◎ **Human Car Wash** (US Patent 3 572 483, issued 1969): Nothing takes up a busy hospital's time more than the washing of patients. Apparently. The 'Human Car Wash' straps dirty types into a harness and moves them from wash station to wash station via conveyor belt . . . first the soapy spray, then the rinser, the dryer and so on. Its ambitious inventor also believes it would prove a huge boon 'to cope with the mass bathing requirements after an atomic bomb'. Indeedy.

◎ **The Kissing Shield** (US Patent 5 787 895, issued 1998): Like to pucker up but not keen on lip-borne diseases? 'The Kissing Shield' stretches a thin latex barrier over a tender moment. Its hopeful inventor stresses the shield is designed for the 'intended recipient of the user's affections'. In other words, there should be no debate about who's packin' the plastic.

◎ **The Life Expectancy Watch** (US Patent 5 130 161, issued 2002): Another corker that has so far failed to attract the kudos it deserves. 'The Life Expectancy Watch' is a personally tailored wrist piece that constantly displays what remains of your likely tenure on earth. Taking into account your genetic background and lifestyle factors, the watch counts backwards, keeping you always appraised of the time you have left and subtly reminding you to make the most of it!

◎ **Toilet Landing Lights** (US Patent 5 263 209, issued 1993): Necessity was surely the mother of this little beauty. Designed to light your way during those otherwise awkward, fumbling midnight toilet stops, the 'Toilet Landing Lights' are waterproof bulbs placed under the rim of the toilet seat that emit a soft, cosmic glow to guide your butt towards its rightful possie.

◎ **Tricycle Lawnmower** (US Patent 4 455 816, issued 1984): Possibly the only way to channel a toddler's boundless energy *and* your need to trim the hedges. DOCS need never know.

These here are crazy times

Who would have thought, as kitchen calendars flipped over to 1900 and Europe was basking in the glow of its own dominance, that the next few decades would see the world almost implode in self-destruction and that a loopy school dropout with a killer sales pitch would lure millions of people to their deaths? Not Britain at any rate, which by this stage was king of the kids and the centrepiece of world trade.

Although Germany and France were obviously up to no good in their secretive bids to mould overseas empires, Britain was far too busy wrapping up the Boer War to notice the Mr Burns-like activities of its neighbours. In fact, Germany was going gangbusters on the development front, creating ever-new applications for its engineering breakthroughs and throwing big bucks at education.

It was in this charged atmosphere that a little-known German physicist having a bad hair life surprised all his co-workers in the Swiss Patent Office by unveiling a riveting paper about relativity. Albert Einstein's complex mathematical formulas made even Isaac Newton's efforts look high school-ish, and it wasn't long before his formulas and theorems were being embraced by scientists the world over. Pity about one of them leading to the atomic bomb, but you get that.

It was also around this time that German physician Sigmund Freud, whose mind was always on the job, discovered man's unconscious brain (down the back of the couch no doubt) and determined the importance of sexuality in shaping one's personality. Perhaps not surprisingly, he freaked plenty of other scientists right out of their rear-fastening pyjamas, and it wasn't until quite a few years later that his theories attracted any merit. Still, it goes to show that one can achieve things even while sitting around thinking about sex all day.

Far removed from all this highfalutin' hypothesising, the average Joe in Europe was suffering. Many families lived below the poverty line, and it was within this context that the idea of international socialism rapidly became the hot topic around water coolers. Paranoia, too, swept the western world as nations increasingly suspected their neighbours of forming devilish alliances and cheating in Immunity Challenges.

A world war probably seemed like a good idea at the time. Certainly, as women and children waved off the millions of men primed to fight for something other than their daily meal ticket, senseless killing may have looked like a wildly romantic proposition and, at the very least, something exciting to fill the next few months. Four years later, with the death toll at ten million, it probably seemed less so.

One of the most significant outcomes of World War I was the repackaging of Uncle Sam—no longer just the big-talkin' rellie no-one wanted to have over for Christmas dinner but rather a diplomatic force of considerable stature. This was not because America offered sage solutions to the troublesome world relationships of the time, but simply because it had cash and loads of it.

Huge loans from the fat cats on Wall Street enabled Europe to accelerate its recovery from the decimation of war, and the US rapidly took on the image of the big kid on the block who was happy to hand out lollies, albeit when it suited him. The world looked on in wonder as America's standard of living continued to skyrocket. They marvelled at guys like Henry Ford, who decided it should be just as easy to make ten thousand cars as it is to make one and pioneered assembly-line processes that put car ownership into the sphere of almost every regular citizen—just reward for their new exciting jobs screwing 378 widgets onto forty-two doo-dats every 19.6 minutes.

But of course it was all too good to last. America's excess and greed tipped the scales on that historically delicate balancing act between success and mediocrity, ultimately leading to the almighty Wall Street crash of 1929; a fall so great it brought all of Europe down with it and plunged the world into economic depression. Good one, Sam.

In fact, greed and excess were only partly to blame for the Great Depression. No historian can fairly leave US President Herbert Hoover off the hook. An outstanding nominee for our Mediocrity Hall of Fame, Hoover (1874–1964) presided over his nation's worst passage in economic history with the kind of blind optimism one can only acquire by having progressed from school dropout to multi-millionaire in a few short chess moves. Even while the nation's financial structures collapsed around his ears, Hoover set about doing what he ultimately become famous for: nothing. Believing that the natural cycles of business would soon lead to an economic upturn, he sat back and watched as more

than twenty-five per cent of all Americans lost their jobs and hundreds of thousands of people became homeless. Poverty-stricken shanty towns became known as 'Hoovervilles', but Hoover himself refused to sanction a program of government works to direct aid to the unemployed.

Ever optimistic, Hoover ran for re-election, but won the votes of only six states against Democrat Franklin Roosevelt. Hoover will be remembered in history as the thirty-fourth most effective US president—a benchmark for George Dubya to shoot for at any rate.

Hardest hit by world recession was Germany, where more than six million people could no longer get a haircut or a real job. Enter stage right, one Adolf Hitler.

Arnold Schwarzenegger notwithstanding, no academically challenged European has made such a dramatic political impact with so little of worth to say. Here, in a truly twisted sense, is history's most telling example of success achieved through mediocrity. Adolf was a school dropout, a failed painter and, as few might know, a man inspired by the writings of officially the worst novelist in all history—Edward Bulwer-Lytton.

Bulwer-Lytton (1803–73) might have fancied himself as a writer, but hundreds of thousands of readers since have deemed his work so bad—his 1830 novel *Paul Clifford* begins with the cliché, 'It was a dark and stormy night'—that an international award for really, really bad writing now exists in his (dis)honour. The Bulwer-Lytton Prize attracts thousands of entries each year, and competition is so hotly contested that only the truly untalented (or the best at mimicking lack of talent) stand a real chance of victory. Last year's winner, Mariann Simms of Alabama, clinched it with the following opening paragraph:

> They had but one last remaining night together, so they embraced each other as tightly as that two-flavour entwined string cheese that is orange and yellowish-white, the orange probably being a bland Cheddar and the white . . . Mozzarella, although it could possibly be Provolone or just plain American, as it really doesn't taste distinctly dissimilar from the orange, yet they would have you believe it does by coloring it differently.

For this dishonour, Edward Bulwer-Lytton shouldn't be turning in his grave (at the end of the day his work has proved far more memorable than that of many of history's most acclaimed writers), but he should perhaps be a tad embarrassed that one of his books, *Reinzi, the last of the tribunes*, greatly inspired one adolescent Adolf Hitler to form a small reading group called the Nazi Party.

Within three years of first spouting his nutty philosophies in a manner worthy of any modern sales industry guru, Adolf had put his money where his moustache was by resurrecting the German army and creating the world's largest air force. By the time he'd poked his stick into the Spanish Civil War and got everyone fired up about socialists and communists, the die had already been cast. In September 1939, Hitler invaded Poland and world peace was all over bar the shouting.

Thirty million or so lives later, Nazism was ultimately defeated, but at a social cost from which the world has never fully recovered. Notwithstanding today's imprisonment of innocent refugees in detention centres and the unsanctioned invasion of nations who really don't have weapons of mass destruction when they say they don't, the horror of concentration camps and Nazi death factories is still almost incomprehensible to modern society.

Individually and collectively, Europe's nations made a surprisingly speedy recovery from the brink of annihilation, though never to the extent where they could rival the world's new obvious superpowers: America and Russia. The so-called Cold War developed into a fascinating, marriage-like ideological tussle that produced some of the world's best spy stories and some of its worst spies. It also produced my favourite oxymoron— military intelligence—and continues to inspire the Secret Squirrel-like activities of nutbags such as Ian Parr; unofficially the world's worst spy and a nominee for our Mediocrity Hall of Fame.

Parr, a forty-six-year-old aircraft engineer who codenamed himself 'Piglet', as you do, was caught red-handed in 2003 trying to pass on secrets about seven top-secret British projects to a Russian agent. At least Piglet *thought* he was a Russian agent. Turns out he worked for MI5. Ironically, Parr had been trying to set himself up a little side-earner business in spying because he feared being made redundant by his employer, British Aerospace. So he availed himself of the company's military secrets and went in search of a cagey Russian type.

Nicknamed 'Hazard' by his former army colleagues, the bumbling, accident-prone father-of-two was celebrating his first major sale of secrets with a pint of lager at his local pub when police swooped on the premises and made their arrest. Devastated at being caught, Parr tried to kill himself while awaiting trial by wiring his spectacles to the prison mains. Fortunately, he only succeeded in burning a scar into his face the exact same shape as his glasses.

But back to history. While America was absorbed in the telly one afternoon in 1957, Russia surprised everyone by launching the first man-made satellite into space. Sputnik 1 was a great success and peeved America no end. Within days, the US government pulled its finger out of its black hole and reignited the space program with a flourish.

All too soon, however, Russia sent up Sputnik III, this time 'manned' with two dogs and about fifty chewed-up sneakers. Then, in a classic stick-that-in-your-pipe-and-smoke-it battle, the Russians sent the first man, Yuri Gargarin, into space, beating America's 1969 moon effort by just twenty-three days. It seemed red rockets really did go faster.

Although no-one could precisely say what the space race was actually for or where indeed the finish line lay, everyone agreed there was no way they could afford to lose it, and the space program quickly became the second most important funding priority of the superpowers after the development of sufficient means to blow the world up seven times over.

Nowadays space missions make for less compelling news and are primarily staged only when world leaders wish to take the focus off their more dastardly endeavours. Case in point: America's landing on Mars in January 2004. Even NASA seemed bored by this uneventful and seemingly inexplicable mission, following up 1969's historic declaration of 'The Eagle has landed' with 'Hey, we're on Mars everybody!' I kid you not. It might as well have been my husband declaring we'd finally made it to the front of the line for the Scooby Doo ride at Movie World.

Ironically, as medical breakthroughs and improved nutritional standards in the 1960s propelled the world's average life expectancy to its highest levels ever, man's innate desire to do himself in became similarly efficient. We plundered the environment like never before, filled the air with industrial carcinogens, distributed handguns like lollies, and accelerated the ongoing development of nuclear weapons.

By the 1980s, western mankind had entered a fairly pessimistic age in history. The inventions and ideas with which we had shaped society now seemed to be shaping us. Our propensity for violence and self-destruction seemed to know no bounds, with murder and drug abuse at unfathomable levels. Overpopulation, pollution, unemployment, poverty and inflation were problems that seemed to swamp any hopes of adequate solutions. And for all our laboratory cleverness, cures for pimples and colds still hopelessly eluded us.

Still, there were always other planets to start afresh on. In 1986 the US National Commission on Space declared that new technology had 'freed mankind to move outward from Earth as a species destined to expand to other worlds'. *We've trashed our place*, the small print read, *can we come to yours?* And such delusion hasn't abated. Even as recently as 2003, George W. Bush revealed that his cosmic vision was to actually send human beings to live on Mars within the next ten years. (Well, you first, Forrest. The rest of us will be right along when you get Foxtel hooked up.)

In the meantime, humans have utilised much of the last fifteen or so years for exploring their 'inner space'—namely their mind and its power to remodel one's personal existence. The 'nihilistic nineties' emerged as a response to both the economic excesses of the eighties (greedy gutses on Wall Street, take another bow) and the growing sense that the world had become so much bigger than the sum of its parts.

The fear of mankind's collective stupidity saw the rise of the more individualised self-help movement—a 'new age' religious-style library of literature and ideas that sought to bring people back in touch with themselves and the things that matter

Mediocrity Hall of Fame
Member: The Church of Scientology

Some new-age religions owe more to mediocrity than they'd care to admit. Certainly, the hundred thousand-plus global devotees of the Church of Scientology seldom discuss the fact that their religion's founder, one L. Ron Hubbard, apparently kickstarted the cult to win a bet.

It's widely reported that Ron accepted a drunken wager from a fellow writer that 'any science fiction hack should be able to create a religion that people will follow en masse'. Ron allegedly upped the stakes by saying that if he hadn't made one million dollars from gullible schmucks within ten years, he'd owe his writer mate $10. In fact, with pithy affirmations such as 'All men shall be my slaves! All women shall succumb to my charms! All mankind shall grovel at my feet and not know why!', Ron made his mill. within three years and the rest is sucked-in history.

A religion based on a gamble on gullibility might not be so silly if its founder wasn't also a raving loon. Many of Hubbard's former colleagues and associates—and even the FBI—have described him as 'unsettled' and even plain 'mental'. Certainly he maintained a tenuous grip on reality at times and an even more tenuous hold on the truth, insisting, for example, that he was trained as an atomic physicist with an honorary PhD. (In fact, he purchased his bogus degree from a diploma mill in California.) He also penned his own recommendation letter in order to receive a berth in the Navy, describing himself as someone who 'has published many millions of words and some fourteen movies'.

Privately, Hubbard married three times and fathered seven children, none of whom he apparently liked very much. His second wife, Sara Northrup, reportedly left him saying that he was a 'paranoid schizophrenic', to which he responded by kidnapping their daughter from the Church of Scientology headquarters in LA and then by kidnapping Sara herself and attempting to declare her insane. Talk about the pot calling the kettle ...

Of course, many scientologists will dispute such history because Hubbard's own biography reads very differently. And hey, why would a science fiction writer make up stuff? But flying in the face of all debate about Hubbard's motives and mentality is the meteoric rise of Scientology, albeit among fickle celebrity types and odd-looking people wielding Dianetics 'stressometers' at market stalls. For sheer numbers alone, Scientology is a huge success story, a masterworks of mediocrity. And it's not so surprising. As Willa Appel wrote in *Cults in America*:

> Ironically, most messiahs have had markedly unstable lives. It is commonplace among them that their calling is precipitated by crisis, nervous breakdown and physical collapse. Most are people who have been unable to successfully integrate themselves into ordinary society. (But) despite their inability to follow the usual routes to success, they manage to create their own.

(i.e. whatever makes you happy, including leaving the wife and kids for your yoga teacher).

Naturally enough, this thinking soon became hijacked by the corporate world, which recognised that self-motivated individuals could do wonderful things to a bottom line. All too quickly, the mini-bar bill at the Hotel of Inner Happiness included fame, fortune, eighty-hour weeks, endless makeovers and a constant sense of emotional inadequacy.

In the twenty-first century, happiness is now consistently redefined to include that which we don't have. What we *do* have has lost its value—relationships are thrown away like doubles tickets at the footy and children are left to raise themselves while their parents try to find the stop button on the treadmill. The vast majority of us live in overcrowded cities trying desperately to avoid each other so as to remain focused on our inadequate selves. Drugs and alcohol seem the only escape from the purpose vacuum we've created—that and televised sport.

With the disturbing rise of terrorism in the modern age, fear is further turning our attention inwards. (I can't change the world, but I can change everything about myself if I hurry.) Suddenly, an ordinary life seems almost lazy and irresponsible, especially when one considers the ever-new possibilities for self-advancement and improvement. Inevitable comparisons with the media's definition of life's 'successful people' leave us hopelessly floundering, and necessitate a life dedicated to personal goals rather than global ones.

In the meantime, the world's resources and potential are being plundered by halfwits and Hollywood. We sense an inexorable movement towards global calamity, but are too busy having our eyebrows waxed to stop it. We believe large-scale change will be enacted by people other than ourselves. By people of greatness.

Yet as this potted history of mankind has shown, greatness and great change more often than not stem from the ordinary. From the mediocre. They happen when ordinary people do ordinary things in large numbers, or when ordinary people do extraordinary things, or when extraordinary things happen to ordinary people. It is only the rear-view mirror of history that makes people and events look bigger than they are.

Yes, the greatest threat to the future of mankind is our growing disregard for ordinary. It has shaped our past and could well make the future a whole lot less stressful if we'd only let it. You don't need to invent something or declare a war or even balance ninety-six milk crates on your head to make history. You just have to show up.

Now go and have a lie-down. That was a big chapter.

Chapter 7

A life more ordinary

Only mediocrity can be trusted to be always at its best.
Sir Max Beerbohm (1872–1956)

I'd never planned on this book entailing so much effort. Originally my idea was to cobble together a few old columns and articles, throw them at a handful of publishers and see who came back with an offer. Like *that* was ever going to work. Only one publisher ultimately got back to me and her summation was this: 'You know, Carrie, I *like* the concept but it needs a little tweaking. Could you possibly, um, rewrite, like, ALL of it?'

'Hell no!' I was about to reply, when suddenly I remembered that having a book published had always been one of my primary goals in life, and that, despite my rudimentary efforts in other areas, it could well end up being the only big goal I ever kicked. And didn't this dovetail nicely into my book concept anyway: if you get a chance to kick a major goal in life, take a giant run-up, but if you don't, and it's just as likely you won't, then hey, don't sweat it?

A lot of the people around you aren't kicking big goals every day, and those that are don't appear to be any happier than you. In fact, some are downright miserable as a result of all that misguided kicking. I think I've been watching too much AFL.

So what started out as a mediocre idea ended up being a book about mediocrity. How brilliant is that? If the book is a best-selling success, then the irony is beautiful, and if it's not, then I can just say 'Well, that's all I ever wanted, *obviously*'.

But if you think the whole mediocrity theme is just a gimmick, just a hook to snag impulse buyers in busy bookshops, then you're wrong. I actually believe wholeheartedly in the philosophy behind this tome, although I have to admit I believe in it even more since writing fifty thousand words about it. Writing is a very introspective sport, and the journey from my first word to the last one has been personally revealing and broadly educational.

I have stumbled across information about myself, about the world around me and about the history of our amazing race that has made me see more clearly the giant hole into which we've all dug ourselves.

I can see, for example, that 'success' has become life's manic greyhound rabbit. It's the moving target we've set for ourselves in the absence of a definitive template on what life is actually *for*. God may have given us rules on how to live, but he was certainly pretty vague on the whole purpose of the gig. And so we have created our own incentives, our own motivations and our own benchmarks with which to fashion a purpose for our existence.

The trouble with this is that we're an innately competitive lot, and when certain benchmarks have been reached by a precious few, we've gone ahead and moved the targets further along. We've done this so often and across so many areas that the whole concept of success has become an entirely fluid, indefinable thing. We'll never achieve it because even if we did, how would we know? There'd all too quickly be a new target to aspire to, a nicer house to own, a richer partner to court, a bigger billboard to occupy. In the meantime life would be throwing us curveball after curveball: sickness, disappointment, poor timing,

dodgy influences, bad advice, rotten luck, a wanker in sales, death, misadventure and a head that isn't getting any more attractive.

No, success is inherently elusive. As is happiness. When asked to define success, most people answer, somewhat insincerely, 'Oh, you know, just being happy'. Sure. Like you, sitting there trying to incite a bidding war between your local pizza deliverers, are radiating success. In reality, up to eighty per cent of the world's population are clinically depressed or, by admission, 'mostly unhappy', and that's just among those of us with two pieces of bread to rub together. Very, very few people would rate themselves as broadly happy, which must surely beg the question: why not?

And my thinking is that the answer to this is buried in the question itself. The reason we're not wildly successful and blissfully happy is because we keep asking ourselves: am I wildly successful and blissfully happy? And because we use other people as our litmus tests; other people who don't know what success and happiness are either. And because we throw millions of dollars each year at an industry that relies on us feeling perennially inadequate and dissatisfied. We buy books, magazines, videos, memberships, endless self-improvement products; we go to courses and seminars; we reinvent ourselves; we change EVERYTHING; all because we've been led to assume we're not good enough as we are. As if managing a life, maintaining relationships, earning a living and resisting the urge to eat Barbecue Shapes until we have to be physically removed from our home isn't all fairly impressive in its own right.

But it's no longer socially acceptable to believe that simply getting by in this crazy game called life is a measure of success in itself. Nor that happiness might be nothing more than cheap laughs off the telly and a late-night run to the servo for double-choc Magnums. And how quickly we forget the lessons of history. History *is* the product of ordinary acts and ordinary people, albeit often in extraordinary circumstances. Certainly, a number of outstanding individuals and overachievers have played their part, but not without the momentum of ordinary humanity rolling them along. Had mankind been anything less than innately ordinary and mediocre, we would have almost certainly self-combusted eons ago. We would have wiped ourselves out, thrown a giant mickey, choked on a bone or outsmarted ourselves well before we realised that the universe doesn't dish out its booty in equal servings. Yes, history is beautiful and revealing when it isn't just about the authors themselves.

I was furious with my father when he first suggested I lower my expectations of life. I automatically assumed he was regretful of his own missed opportunities and happy to see me simply settle. I have since recognised that he *did* want me to have it all in life, but he also wanted me to be happy about *not* having it all. Because that's what ninety-nine per cent of us end up with. We end up with life's standard issue: a handful of people who care about us, a few randomly timed opportunities, a cupful of luck, indescribable moments of bliss, and loads and *loads* of challenges. And all the positive thinking and deep breathing in the world isn't going to change any of that. It's okay. It's cool. It's ordinary.

So anyway. For mine, it pays to think of life as a movie set. You've got the stars of the show—the beautiful, fortunate few who command the camera's attention and are born to be remembered. You've got the extras—those with a requisite amount of talent and ambition; who are happy to turn up and hang out and who get to be in the movie without having to put up with any of the pressure that the stars do. And you've got the devastated also-rans—those almost-beautiful, less-fortunate ones who've worked so hard to get to the top that they've lost sight of everything important along the way, and who resent their successful counterparts so much they'll happily change everything about themselves to get a better shot at success next time; at any cost.

Now we can't all be stars, and according to most reports being a star is not all it's cracked up to be anyway, so being an extra is clearly the only sensible option here. But maybe that's just my interpretation. Certainly, the appeal of the modern self-help industry and indeed of reality TV would seem to suggest that many, many people would rather sacrifice everything to become a star, even though most of them will hopelessly over- or undershoot the mark, miss the target completely and wish they'd taken the time instead to have kids, to make popcorn and to develop a personality. Economics' Law Of Diminishing Returns almost certainly applies to life when you observe the unhappiness of so many ostensibly successful people. The biggest stars don't fade out, they implode.

But there wouldn't *be* great movies without extras! And it's not unheard of for a diligent extra to be plucked from obscurity and skyrocketed to stardom without even having to go through the effort of acting school, botox and the casting couch. Extras earn a good solid wage for decent, half-fun work and an average amount of kudos. On a pound-for-pound basis, what could be a better option?

The biggest stars don't fade out, they implode.

But this is not a class action against effort. Not making an effort gets you nowhere in life, royalty notwithstanding. But at the same time, putting in a ridiculous amount of effort might also get you nowhere. So isn't the safest bet to put in a modicum of effort and hope for good things?

In doing so, you should also consider yourself one of the most important contributors to our society. Because irrefutably, mediocrity is a huge income-producer. Countless occupations and industries rely desperately on the mediocre efforts of ordinary individuals. Where would fix-it companies, rescue teams, editors, smash repairers, rehab consultants, counsellors, firemen, cleaners, solicitors, personal trainers and those guys who (allegedly) try to find everything you've lost on your computer be without random acts of ordinariness?

And of course where would the multi-million-dollar self-help industry be without ordinary? Or more accurately, where would it be if we didn't all believe, for all the wrong reasons, that ordinariness is somehow not good enough for this world? Obviously it would fall over tomorrow, though not before throwing a giant pair of Chinese stress balls at whoever moved its cheese. (Incidentally, if this book happens to help you in any way, I can't be held responsible for that.)

But perhaps this wouldn't be such a bad thing if a new industry emerged in its place; one trading in hearty backslaps and routine shrugs of the shoulder. The self-*justification* industry would see the emergence of a new compelling section of the bookstore, one with titles such as *Feel the fear and back right off*, *The four or five or so habits of consistently adequate people* and *Who ate the dip?* 'Corporate retreat' would be a term used to describe employees allowed to go home early because they've finished all their work and would rather not spend the rest of the day pretending to be productive while their kids are in after-school care. The world's 'rich list' would exempt those who are also miserable and unfulfilled.

You know, I wish I had said all this to the fellow author I met at my publisher's Christmas party last year. When put on the spot to explain my book concept, I simply coughed up: 'Well, I guess you could say it's a piss-take of the self-help movement. Ha ha! What's yours about?'

'Well, I guess you could say it's a self-help book', he answered, deadpan.

But then, why pass up such a beautifully mediocre moment?

A life more ordinary: the cheat's guide

If you couldn't be bothered reading this book, what with all the pages and turning and stuff, below is a guts-at-a-glance summary to help you take those first mediocre steps towards a more blissfully ordinary life. Why not group email it to ten people you couldn't be bothered contacting personally?

Work: Karma does not exist in the workplace. If you give a talentless, manipulative, grossly unfair boss enough rope, he'll simply hang more people.

Delegate: Remember, a job worth doing is worth contracting out.

Good health: Given that most serious health crises happen to people when they least expect them, it's good practice to imagine the worst. So yes, it's probably a tumour.

Achievement: If at first you don't succeed, try, try, try something else. Or don't. Whatever.

Jetsetting: Don't be conned by airline advertising that boasts a crash-free safety record. It just means they're due.

Parenting: It's best to view parenting like a sort of long-term lay-by plan that takes so long to pay off, you forget why you wanted it in the first place. Having said that, there is nothing in life so rewarding and satisfying as a child's unconditional love. It's just a shame it doesn't last beyond the move to solids.

Hard work: Make hay while the supervisor's watching.

Exercise: Everyone knows that a healthy body equals a healthy mind, and vice-versa. Watch as many aerobics and yoga videos as you can. I like to put them on when I'm ironing.

Love: Pick someone. Make it work.

Challenge: As Nike says, just do it. Unless of course you don't really want to.

Enlightenment: Buy every self-help book available. Pile them on top of each other and place a nice piece of Tassie Oak on the top. Wa-la! Coffee table.